The Economics of Energy

The
Economics of
ENERGY

What Went Wrong?

ROGER LeROY MILLER

William Morrow & Company, Inc.
New York   1974

Contents

Preface

Not many economists were very interested in the field of energy during the fifties. In the sixties, we started changing a little bit because it became obvious to certain interested parties that things weren't as they should be in the energy field. Then in the seventies the picture changed completely. Now everybody is interested in energy. The big blackout on the East Coast a few years ago made me, as well as millions of other people, aware of the fact that something was going wrong. While the sociologists tried to figure out why birth rates in New York City increased nine months after the blackout, economists as well as scientists and engineers tried to figure out how to prevent such disasters in the future.

I became associated with a consulting firm specializing in energy economics several years ago. For the year and a half that this association lasted, I was introduced into not only the colorful terminology of the energy business (load shedding, shaving, and other equally fascinating words), but also to the complex, real world problems of regulation and competition in this field. I also gained a tremendous amount of schooling about the social costs of market solutions from my associates, in particular Irwin M. Stelzer and Bruce C. Netschert. After reading this book, they may say that I didn't learn my lessons well enough; nonetheless, I am grateful for the insights obtained from them.

For several years now I have been teaching a seminar on the economics of ecology. Increasingly in these seminars, I have covered topics relating to the energy crisis. My students have "kept me honest" by pointing out many implications of my policy making suggestions that I did not touch on. I am equally grateful to these students for their tenacity.

Since this short book is meant for the largest audience possible, I have spared my readers the pain of having to wade through specialized jargon that is comprehensible only to my colleagues. Also, I must warn the reader that to some extent I have overstepped my bounds as a professional economist and injected some social and political judgments of my own with respect to the causes, effects, and future of our energy problems. Strictly speaking, economists aren't supposed to utter anything but positive, value-free economics. I agree, but see nothing wrong with presenting personal (value-laden) views of problems if they are so labelled. My values will be obvious to the reader, even if sometimes they aren't labelled in bold letters.

A number of people helped me in the preparation of this book. I wish to thank in particular my colleagues Yoram Barzel and Eugene Silberberg, who commented on various drafts of the manuscript. Susan Vita Miller gave in at the last minute and helped me smooth out the rough spots. My secretary, Ms. Georgiana Schuder, as always, efficiently handled the burden of typing the various drafts in record time. Unfortunately, due to the energy crisis, my office was not heated on the weekends and the consequent cold she caught while working delayed final manuscript completion for some time.

Is nothing sacred?

RLM

Seattle, 1974

CHAPTER 0

A Fairy Tale

Once upon a time, there was a great land that was inhabited by only a few peaceful natives who lived in harmony with nature. They took only what they needed from the land. They engaged in no unnecessary destruction of living things. They killed only to eat. They built only to provide shelter. They clothed themselves only with essentials.

For many, many moons, the natives remained undisturbed by the outside world. One day, however, foreigners invaded their land. Peace was no longer possible. Soon, the foreigners began arriving in droves—thousands upon thousands upon thousands. These people had a different idea about life. As they continued to increase in number and multiply throughout the land, they engaged in sometimes wanton destruction of that which nature so abundantly provided. They cut down trees and did not replant them. They dug up coal and left the remains scattered around, preventing plant life from ever growing again. They used more and more of the resources available. They went forth and still begat and still multiplied. Soon they inhabited every corner of that great land. They had become rich, rich indeed. They had great factories providing products unheard of ever before. They sought the easy life where everything was done for them. Soon, however, problems began to arise.

The inhabitants of this land began to notice a strange phenomenon. The air in the cities blackened. The water became fouled. The newly paved streets were overcrowded. The sidewalks could hold no more people. Little by little, a few people started to cry out in despair: "Wait, wait, we can consume no longer, for we are destroying the very basis of life—the environment in which we live!" But these people were ignored, or only given lip service. The problems continued to increase. The population continued to expand. Soon key resources began to run out. But everybody said, "So what? We'll find something else."

Then it happened—the year that no one can forget. The land ran out of energy sources! Of course, people could still walk and there was a little bit of electricity available from dams and rushing water. And a few smart people had even turned to wind power or had tapped the stream in the ground. But that was trivial compared to the needs of the nation. Then, when all of the energy sources ran out, the nation turned into one dim, noisy sea of complaining humanity. The cars did not run, the lights did not glow, the houses were not heated.

We had exhausted Nature's cornucopia.

CHAPTER 1

The Day of Reckoning
Has Arrived (According to Some)

That fairy tale you just read sounds pretty outrageous, doesn't it? Well, it doesn't to everybody. We are being increasingly told that the day of reckoning is upon us, not because we have sinned morally, but because we have consumed excessively. The energy crisis is seen by many as merely further indication that the well has run dry. Over-rich Americans can no longer keep consuming at past rates. Growth must come to a standstill if we are to survive on a planet with limited resources. This may have been the country of abundance before, but it no longer is. The Zero Economic Growth advocates are now having a field day. The number of "I told you so's" has now entered the 27,000,000 bracket.

Not too long ago, a group of researchers presented a report for the Club of Rome's project on the predicament of mankind. This well-publicized, widely-read book, *The Limits of Growth*, shows all doubting Thomases that before the year 2100, the world as a system will reach a point where the population can no longer be supported by existing resources. According to the study, sufficient pollution controls, better birth control, and other short-run stop-gap measures will not prevent us from running out of food. Of course, Malthus told us that many, many years ago. He didn't tell us we'd run out of energy, though, and neither did the MIT computer used for the mathematical forecasts presented in *Limits*.

Doomsdayers will say, "So what?" That just means that the equations will have to be rearranged. The end has to come about some day, according to ZEGers, because we are not learning to live with our scarce resources. In other words, if we're not willing to accept a reduction in our consumption habits, we're doomed. Just look at the energy problem.

The energy problem, of course, is not new. In one of Nixon's numerous forays against the press, he pointed out very clearly that he had been the first president to ever send an energy message to Congress, and he did that during his first administration. Now you might be asking yourself how one comes up with an idea that there's going to be an energy problem if none exists at the time. The answer is easy. You simply project what people need into the future, project what the economy is going to supply, and come up with the difference, called an energy deficit. Then you look around you and ask some experts to give you some other estimates: how many years' oil reserves do we have? Only 10? Help! What's the problem with natural gas? Not enough? Help! How about electricity? Brownouts? Blackouts? Help! The problem or crisis was in the offing for a number of years already. All it took was something unusual to push us over the brink.

Unfortunately, nobody seems to have sat down and looked at the facile doomsday arguments very carefully. When doomsdayers Meadows and Meadows put out *The Limits to Growth*, the world shuddered. Finally, though, a few people realized that they'd heard that story before and it never came true. Ah, but today is different. Maybe so, maybe not. Additionally, other students of the problem realized that there was something strangely mechanical about the equations fed into the MIT computer. Why did everything except technology grow geometrically? How come in the Club of Rome models there was no account taken of how the signals to economic agents change as the situation changes? Won't there be any changing signals to us which will lead to changing resource use rates?

In spite of such real questions about doomsday models, prophets of an energy shortage have convinced the vast majority of people that only drastic measures can save us from disaster. For the next couple of years, everybody is supposed to be willing to sacrifice a little bit so that all may benefit. Presumably the hope is that more permanent solutions will come up and energy will no longer be a problem. There are skeptics, though, and they're the ones who are firmly convinced that the only solution is no growth: cut out frivolous consumption of energy; change life styles; get back to nature; become self-sufficient again, in energy as well as other things; don't rely on the rest of the world, make it on your own; and if you do it right, we might, with a little help from up above, survive.

Right off the bat, you ought to know something. Doomsdayers have constructed models of the world which are neither supported by history nor by any theory consistent with the way you and I act in our day to day behavior. And when these doomsday advocates get on the energy kick, the same thing holds. We do have problems, of that there is little doubt. But you'll see in the following few pages that many, if not most, of these problems were created by naive, inept, or devious political entrepreneurs. You'll see, for example, that the big oil scare could have been avoided, or at the very least could have had many fewer disruptive effects on the American as well as the world economy. You'll also see that an incredible number of deleterious implications of current policy solutions, both real and proposed, have never been touched on by policy makers. It's about time someone gave the other side of the story.

Why don't we start by examining the oil problems. And what better way than to see what oilmen have been doing all this time.

CHAPTER 2

A Country that Runs on Oil Can't Afford to Run Short

The title of this chapter was taken from an advertisement paid for by the oil companies of America. You should be suspicious of it then, and you have every right to be. You expect oil companies to further their own best interests, and that's what they've been doing (with the help of the government) for a number of years now. It's cost you and me a mint. Let's look at some of the gimmicks that have caused higher oil prices in the past. The most egregious has probably been the oil import program.

Back in the early 1950s, oil company executives started to notice how foreign competition was causing oil prices to fall, or at least not to rise as high as the American companies would have liked them to. While U.S. oil companies were running into rising costs to get out more oil, immense reserve discoveries were made at this time in the Mideast. The U.S., for the first time, was becoming a net importer of oil. So a plan was worked out. The oil companies got their lobby to convince the people around President Eisenhower that we should restrict, for reasons of national security, the amount of imported foreign crude oil. That's right—for national security. The reasoning went as follows: In time of war, our foreign supplies of oil would probably be cut off. If this were the case and we did not have adequate supplies at home, we would be in serious strategic trouble. A basic input into the defense machine— petroleum products—would be in short supply. Hence, if we were to restrict the amount of foreign oil that could enter the U.S., there would be an incentive for American companies to do more exploration and we would be better off in case of war when our supply lines might be broken. Otherwise stated, if we use up more of our oil today by importing less, we will be better off in the case of war. Pretty good reasoning, right? Well absurd as it was, nobody seemed to doubt it, least of all Eisenhower. There began a voluntary oil importation restriction system which, as all voluntary systems have a tendency to do, broke down. Foreign crude was at that time cheaper than American crude. Hence, there was an incentive to import from other countries and refine here. When the voluntary plan broke down, Eisenhower issued a second voluntary program in 1957. When it, too, failed to curb imports, he issued a proclamation on March 10, 1959 placing oil imports under mandatory controls, and the oil import quota system became a law, which was probably unconstitutional, but which no one tested in court.

In the beginning, an Oil Import Administration was set up. Each year it determined the total quantity of crude oil that could be imported. Permission to import was granted on the basis of current refining output and of importing activities for the late 1950s. Special tickets authorized the importation of a specific number of barrels of oil.

Once obtained, these tickets for imported crude oil could be traded in exchange for other crude oil products. It's easy to figure out why such trading would have taken place. A barrel of imported foreign crude used to sell for as much as $1.25 less than domestic. Given the choice, any domestic refinery was obviously willing to pay for the right to buy foreign crude at the lower price. Since the tickets generally were not allowed to be bought and sold outright, they were used as a medium of exchange. Companies wishing to import crude oil and lacking authorization implicitly paid as much as $1.25 for a ticket which gave them the right to import one barrel of foreign crude oil. Who benefitted from such a program? Well, it depended on who got the tickets. Who got the tickets typically followed company size lines, although a sliding scale was used to help out small refineries. In general, though, the larger the company, the greater the number of tickets received. Since they were each worth approximately $1.25, big companies found themselves with tremendous windfall gains, medium companies enjoyed moderate gains, and small companies were left out in the cold. In total, ticket holders got a $1,000,000 a day subsidy! Essentially the stockholders in the lucky companies were treated to a net worth increase as soon as the oil import quota system was understood. Most of the lucky companies ended up being local producers, not importers.

Now, how did the oil import quota system affect you the consumer? What it did was reduce the supply of crude oil available in the United States. With any given demand for a product, be it crude oil, shoes, or electric vibrators, a reduction in supply means a higher price. What happened, then, was that crude oil prices were artificially high for a number of years until the world price exceeded the domestic price. During this period, consumers were shelling out $4 to $5 billion a year annually in the form of higher prices for gasoline, heating oil, and other petroleum products. The people who collected this money were essentially the stockholders in the companies that received the oil import tickets. The oil industry succeeded in hoodwinking the American public and the government into accepting the national defense argument in order to keep the price of oil products higher than would have obtained in an unrestricted situation.

If in fact the national defense argument held any water at all, it did not necessarily require an oil import quota system. The Department of Defense could have and still can store as much oil as it feels appropriate to take account of possible supply line interruptions during an all-out war. In 1969, a Bureau of Mines study showed what the cost would be of assuring a 12 month supply of crude oil. The study figured that at the rate of 8 million barrels a day in 1975, it would cost about $700 million a year for the 1971-1980 period, if the oil were stored in underground salt domes. Other alternatives mentioned in the study were federal investment of several hundred million dollars over the next decade to achieve shale oil production of one million barrels daily by 1980, or a similar investment to produce the same amount of oil from coal by 1980.

In other words, we have lots of alternatives to assure ourselves of adequate oil during times of war. We can store it underground or above ground in steel tanks. The underground storage could be in the previously-mentioned salt domes, or in artificially created underground caverns. Another alternative is the creation of oil fields that are shut down to be used only when imports become unavailable. A later study has shown that it would cost us about 50 to 75 cents per barrel to store an amount equal to a two years' supply of imported oil. This seems a lot cheaper than the alternatives suggested and the ones used. The oil import quota system could have been scrapped or never started to begin with, and the notion of total self-sufficiency, which we'll discuss later, isn't necessary either.

Moreover, the American taxpayer can be given an exact estimate of the resource cost to him of having enough oil in case of war. This should be included in the Defense Department budget for everyone to see, instead of using roundabout, inefficient, and expensive alternatives that hide the cost in the form of higher oil product prices to consumers.

The same is true for all other economic pieces of legislation ostensibly passed for national security reasons. If the taxpayer knows the true cost of national security, he can make a better judgment about what he's willing to pay. It would also enable generals—who are, after all, our military experts—to determine what is needed for security rather than having the oil industry teaching them and us about national security. The oil industry has been taking us for a ride for a long time.

The story doesn't end here, however, for the oil industry, that champion of free enterprise and capitalism, has succeeded in getting numerous other special benefits, all designed to subsidize the industry. In the past, the oil industry has been induced to use larger than economically efficient amounts of resources because of special tax stimuli: depletion allowances, full costing of dry wells, capital gains tax privileges, etc. Let's look at the infamous depletion allowances first.

Since the amount of oil found in each pocket is eventually going to be depleted by the pump over it, owners of producing wells can opt for a special tax program whereby they are allowed percentage depletion deductions when computing their taxes. To understand this practice, you have to understand that when a businessman buys a machine, he is allowed to deduct from his income the cost of the depreciation of that machine each year. Hence, he pays no tax on that amount of income. Similarly, an oil man deducts a percentage of the depletion of his oil well.

Currently, he can deduct 22 percent of the gross value of the oil at the well head, but before 1970 the figure was 27 percent. Now why would an oil man prefer this scheme to the regular cost depreciation schedule applied by most businessmen for depreciation of normal machinery?

Look at it this way. If you pay $5 million for a machine, the total depreciation you can claim will never exceed $5 million. On the other hand, if you have an oil well that cost you $5 million and you opt for percentage depletion, you may in fact be able to deduct more than $5 million. Why? Simply because the 22 percent depletion allowance can be used every year forever. The total amount depleted may far exceed the actual amount spent on digging the well. The depletion allowance is based on the *value* of the crude, not on *actual* expenses.

Contrary to popular belief, though, it appears that even when oil men could use the higher 27 percent depletion allowances legally in force before 1970, this tax provision did not lead to truly excessive use of resources in domestic oil exploration. It is only when the controversial percentage depletion tax gimmick is heaped on top of the other oil industry tax advantages that the full story becomes clear. In oil exploration, an unfortunate fact of life is that not all of the drilled wells end up as gushers. In fact, approximately 80 percent of all drilled wells end up being dry. Then they are called dry holes. Since wet wells cannot be found, however, without hitting some dry ones, the implicit or true cost of a wet well must also include the cost of a proportionate number of dry holes. That is, on average the true cost of finding one producing well in the U.S. also includes the cost of drilling four dry holes.

However, the Internal Revenue Service seems to think along somewhat different lines. It permits the costs of all dry wells to be deducted from other income. If you happen to be in the upper tax brackets and are a partner in an oil exploration syndicate, you can deduct your part of the dry hole costs from your ordinary income. If, for example, your marginal tax bracket is 70 percent, every dollar you spend for dry hole exploration ends up costing you only 30¢.

In addition to the dry hole tax provision,.exploration firms which sell wet wells are required to pay only the capital gains rate on the difference between the selling price and the total calculated costs of the wet well. (Remember that the dry holes' costs have already been deducted from other income.)

The oil explorer gets a double benefit: he can apply the lower capital gains tax rate to the net income from the sale of his wet wells; *and* he can also get the benefit of a higher kickback by applying the cost deduction of dry holes to his other income, which is necesarily taxed at a higher than capital gains rate. Moreover, in addition to writing off the cost of all dry holes in the year they are drilled, explorers can do the same to a large portion of the cost of successful wells. Intangible drilling costs (IDCs), which include such costs as labor, etc., as opposed to pipe costs, comprise about 70 percent of the cost of a wet well and all IDCs are deductible in the year incurred. Thus, an oil company can plan its annual budget so as to pay zero taxes without planning to drill all dry wells.

Depletion allowances, full costing of dry wells off other income, capital gains concessions, and the IDC deduction are not given to the oil industry at a zero cost to the economy. The end result of these tax gimmicks has been an inefficient use of resources in domestic oil development. In the past, when we had higher marginal tax brackets, lower capital gains rates, and higher depletion allowances, the estimate was that the use of resources was sometimes 250 percent higher than it would have been without these gimmicks.

Of course, if all that wasn't enough, the oil industry, at least in several areas of the United States, has arranged for government enforcement of cartel allocation restrictions. Have you ever heard of the Texas Railroad Commission? Probably not, and you probably would guess it has something to do with railroads. Well, it doesn't. What it has to do with is setting production quotas for wells. On what grounds, you might be asking. Well, conservation is probably a good guess, but the true grounds are quite different and quite obvious. In the past, before the recent oil problems, domestic companies found that as they increased production, price would eventually fall. They didn't like that, and therefore a number of regions in the United States, at the implicit or explicit behest of oil interests, formed commissions such as the Texas Railroad Commission, to regulate the production of existing oil wells. What does this mean?

This means that we have a cartel arrangement supported by government agencies with the legal power to prevent cheating. To make matters worse, Congress passed a law—the "Oil Compact"—which makes it easier for individual states to get together to "coordinate" their efforts.

Recently the Texas Railroad Commission has set the production quotas at 100 percent of capacity, as you might well expect. But in the past, when the rates have been very low, production was set considerably below full capacity. Not only did this mean higher prices for oil products bought by consumers, but it also led to additional inefficiencies because there was a minimum amount of production that every well was allowed, thus encouraging oil companies to drill more wells than they would have otherwise.

Now take a second look at the wonderfully competitive free enterprise oil industry in the United States. True, it's competitive, so long as the government doesn't step in and foster cartel arrangements such as it does by the use of prorationing schemes which keep prices up. An obvious policy decision that could be effected without very much opposition at all from taxpayers would be the elimination of special privileges to the oil industry and the elimination of legal cartel monitoring arrangements in the form of agencies such as the Texas Railroad Commission. Now, you might cry, "No, certainly not now. What we want is more oil, not less." That's true, but we don't have to have it come out of the ground in an inefficient manner. The way to get more oil from the oil industry is to let it respond to higher prices, which it is obviously doing. It does not need an additional impetus from special subsidies which cause an inefficient use of resources.

CHAPTER 3

On Giving the World
Oil Monopoly an Even Break

In late '73 there was another war in the Middle East, wasn't there? Again, the Arab countries didn't get the land concessions they wanted. So what did they do? They used oil politics to bring pressure to bear on other countries who presumably would become less sympathetic to the Israeli cause. The result, according to most observers, was an oil crisis, and, hence, an energy crisis in the U.S. and abroad. In a few short weeks, 10 to 15 percent of the U.S.'s crude oil supply dried up. But was it really caused by the Arab-Israeli War? In other words, are we to blame that unfortunate belicose action for our energy crisis? Perhaps, but not completely. We must realize that it was also due to the incredible bungling of our State Department, with the help of other governments, that we got into the mess to begin with. To fully understand that, you have to be aware of the economics behind the world oil cartel.

In the first place, that world oil cartel has been around for a long time. But you never heard of it, did you? The reason you never heard of it was that until recently, it wasn't very effective. A cartel is only effective if it can

27

restrict production; otherwise, it has no effect whatsoever. The Persian Gulf oil producing countries wanted to extract monopoly profits out of their black gold a long time ago. Unfortunately, there were always chiselers on any agreement. After all, the incentive to chisel is always there. That's the nature of the economic beast, whether he be here or abroad. Moreover, the world's oil supply doesn't all reside under the sands of the Middle East. A lot of it is found in Africa and elsewhere. But even if it weren't the case, the analysis would still hold. The only way to extract monopoly profits is to have a monopoly, and the only way you can have a monopoly is by making sure that nobody cheats on a cartel agreement. Once you do that, you can get everybody to cut back the supply they are providing. That's the only way you can keep the price up because you can't sell the same quantity of anything (just about) at a higher price if nothing else changes.

Getting back to the world cartel. Back in 1960, an organization began called OPEC, or Organization of Petroleum Exporting Countries. It includes Abu Dhabi, Algeria, Indonesia, Iran, Iraq, Kuwait, Lybia, Nigeria, Qatar, Saudi Arabia, and Venezuela (and recently Ecuador). When it came into existence, its purpose was obviously to maximize the benefits from owning oil for its members. It couldn't do much during the sixties because there seemed to be an ever-expanding supply that was keeping ahead of demand. As demand grew, new discoveries expanded supply so fast that wellhead prices for crude oil actually fell slightly from 1960 to 1970. Then in 1970 and 1971, the rate of growth of the demand actually slowed down. So it seems unpredictable that the cartel would have really got going at that time. But it did, and in part its new power was caused by some, unwise and unfounded interventions on the part of the U.S. State Department. State convened representatives of all importing nations in Paris in 1970 after Lybia and the Persian Gulf countries had already raised crude oil prices fairly dramatically in a very short period of time. It appears that State thought this type of aggressive behavior indicated there was a threat of an oil embargo, so it convinced other countries at the Paris meeting that it was in everyone's best interests to agree to the price rises.

The Persian Gulf nations saw a good thing coming. Our cowardice resulted in the threat of an embargo unless prices were increased again. What did we do? We attended the Tehran and Tripoli conferences where agreements were signed in 1971 which granted all exporting oil countries in OPEC huge increases in their take per barrel of crude oil. These agreements were signed by all OPEC members and by many oil companies, including American ones. In essence, however, it was the governments of the importing countries who were signing those agreements. We were at the head of the list. Why did we do this? Who knows. According to State Department insiders, it was in the hope that Persian Gulf solidarity would bring world peace and with it, stable crude oil prices. In fact, the U.S. State Department issued a statement saying that the international oil business was entering an era of good feeling, one of stability that would last at least five years. Ho, ho, ho.

The State Department ignored some basic economics. You can't raise prices unless you have a monopoly. You can't have an effective cartel unless it's got some way to prevent people who are in the cartel from cheating. All that the importing nations had to do when they got together in Paris was to tell OPEC "no go," instead of ratifying the suggested price increases. An agreement among the importing nations could have countered any OPEC monopoly power. For example, one suggestion that MIT economist M.A. Adelman puts forth is that importing countries can make selling agreements among the various companies. In other words, all oil companies agree to sell crude oil to any other company which OPEC members might shut down. The crude is sold to the shut down company at cost plus taxes. This way, shutting down any particular oil company within the OPEC region would not affect to any great extent world oil supplies. In this way, OPEC would know that it couldn't pressure importing countries, that it did not, have much monopoly powers. In fact, we see this in the admission of the Shah of Iran who said in 1971, "If the oil producing countries suffer even the slightest defeat, it would be the death knell for OPEC, and from then on the countries would no longer have the courage to get together." Unfortunately, the importing countries, with the U.S. at the helm of the ship, gave in without so much as a fist fight.

Surprisingly enough, underdeveloped countries have been cheering the OPEC countries on; the Arab nations are considered part of the Third World, too. As MIT's Adelman further pointed out, it's the underdeveloped countries that certainly are hurt as much or more than anyone by high oil prices, but they don't say a word.

Let's look at this situation a little more carefully. Did OPEC need the '73 Israeli-Arab War to cut off production and raise prices? In a way it did, but not for the reasons you think. It was planning to raise prices anyway, and of course the only way it could keep those prices up was to restrict the output of the various member countries. As output is restricted more and more, prices rise higher and higher; however, the incentive to cheat becomes unbearable. Sooner or later such an arrangement has to fail. This last time it was Iran that broke the agreement almost from the very beginning and was supplying oil at the going price to whomever would pay for it.

You have to realize that as the price rises, other countries not members of the cartel have an incentive to increase shipments. But as those shipments increase, it takes further reductions in the production of the OPEC companies to keep the price up. Sooner or later something has to give, and something of course has to give when you consider that it costs at most less than a dollar, and perhaps not much more than 10 to 40¢, to produce a barrel of crude oil in the Middle East. Compare that to the $4, $5, $8, $9, $10 or whatever price that was being charged for Arab oil after the war. When what you're selling yields you ten times its cost in revenues, that's a pretty high profit, and one you would certainly like to get on an expanding volume, right? But all along the cartel is telling you to cut back production so as to keep the price up. The '73 war turned out to be an excuse to do what OPEC was going to do anyway. What it did was provide the glue to hold the cartel intact; the chiselers had a harder time chiseling. The oil industry has thought all along, and continues to think, that the OPEC cartel will eventually collapse because that glue has got to crack sometime. Most knowledgeable oil men give the cartel no more than three years.

Now you know why we're bothering to get oil out of Alaska and the North Sea even though it's costing considerably more than it costs to bring it out of the Arabian desert—because we gave in to the OPEC cartel such that world oil prices are high enough to make this very expensive Alaskan and North Sea oil worth getting. From a world-wide efficiency basis, it's ridiculous to spend the resources to bring that oil into the world at all today. We should first be using up that really cheap oil in the Middle East. But so long as OPEC remains firm, that cheap oil is going to be selling at 10 to 20 times its cost. OPEC pricing and production restricting tactics, however, will ultimately lead to its demise. Soon new sources of oil and other energy sources will be supplying more and more fuel in response to these high prices. Then there's going to be a chiseler, OPEC will break down, and the world price of oil will plummet. You can bet on that, unless human nature has changed in the last year and chiseling no longer occurs.

Many of the State Department people who were involved in the oil dealings made a lot of long-term projections. They were and still are convinced that we're going to have to import huge quantities of foreign oil in the not-too-distant future in order to meet our energy needs. For example, according to James E. Atkins of the State Department, an adequate supply of oil for the U.S. depends on Saudi Arabia's, for example, meeting its 1980 production goal of 20 million barrels a day, more than a three--fold increase over its 1972 output. Presumably this would mean so much money in foreign exchange that the Arab nation, as well as other Arab nations, won't know what to do with it.

This is a great point to make these days.* What can the Arabs do with all that money they're going to make? Presumably very little. That's why they can supposedly keep their cartel together, because they don't need the money. This is the same as saying that you don't need the money from another job because you don't have any time to spend it since you're working so much. Don't you have an option? Can't you make more money today, save it, and spend it when you stop working so hard? Don't the Arabs have an option? Can't they make huge fortunes from their oil, invest the money everywhere they want so that they can live off the interest forever and ever? Certainly they have this option. That's why it's ridiculous to think that they won't respond to the possibility of cheating on the cartel and making more money in so doing.

---

*And a strange one. Arab nations seem to be acting like they want as much money as possible.

You also have to realize that we're extracting a very small percentage every year of total *proven* world reserves. The latest estimate is that we're taking out less than 3 percent, which isn't very much. Now of course, even at 3 percent a year, with a fixed amount of reserves we'd eventually run out. A funny thing, though, happened on the way to the forum. Reserves are greater today than they were in 1935, even though we've consumed much more oil than we ever thought we would. But how could this be, you might ask. Easy. Proven reserves mean just that— reserves known and proven and available at current market prices for oil. As the price goes up, more reserves are found. As technology changes, more reserves become provable because they can be profitably taken out of the ground. Of course, that still doesn't mean we have enough oil to last us from here to eternity. At any rate of use, no matter how small, we will eventually run out if nature isn't forming any new oil. But that's just a truism, no more relevant than observing that inflation means rising prices. Look at the accompanying table, the data of which was taken from the *Oil and Gas Journal.* The Middle East in 1972 was pulling out of the ground a lower percentage of its proven resources than anywhere else in the world except China and Western Europe.

Oil is just one form of energy. We also have to look at natural gas, coal, uranium, and to a much lesser extent, geothermal, solar, and wind power. The question is not "Are we running out of oil?" and not even "When will we run out of oil?" but, rather, "Is there anything we're doing wrong today that makes us use our various energy sources in inappropriate manners?" Conservation of energy sources is an important issue, but certainly not the key issue at stake in analyzing the current oil situation. That situation was caused by a number of factors, not the least being the ineptness of State Department officials in getting oil com-

Table 1

	Proven Reserves (millions of barrels)	Percent of World Total	1972 production (millions of barrels)	Production as percent of reserves
MIDDLE EAST	355,852	53.3	6,611	1.9
AFRICA	106,402	15.9	2,172	2.0
U.S.S.R.	75,000	11.2	2,876	3.8
U.S.	36,823	5.5	3,455	9.4
SOUTH AMERICA	27,782	4.2	1,540	5.5
CHINA	19,500	2.9	186	1.0
CANADA	10,200	1.5	554	5.4
INDONESIA	10,005	1.5	387	3.9
WESTERN EUROPE	8,582	1.3	113	1.3
OTHER	16,737	2.5	674	4.0
TOTAL	666,883	100.0	18,568	2.8

panies to sign the Tehran and Tripoli agreements. To top it all off, Washington created just the right kind of public relations to encourage the kind of blackmail we've been subjected to by OPEC.

Look at it this way. What is the worst thing you could do if you truly were dependent on a very small number of suppliers of a crucial product? Obviously, the worst thing you could do is let those very few suppliers know how much you really depended on them, because once they know that they've got you where they want you, they're certainly going to exploit the situation. But what did our government actually do? It set up an incredible public relations effort to make everybody in the world think that we were totally dependent on Arab oil. That doesn't happen to be the case since we only import 10 to 15 percent of our total oil supply from the Middle East. Nonetheless, we gave that impression, and in so doing encouraged OPEC to act in the blackmailing fashion in which it has.

Moreover, government acquiescence to special interest pressure by the oil industry has for many years now cost consumers a high price, as we plainly saw in the last chapter. Can the same be said of electricity? Obviously something must be said about that precious energy source, because we are facing electricity crises all the time now.

Read on.

CHAPTER 4

The Blackout Blues

Singing the blues today sometimes means singing in the dark. Those of you who experienced the biggest blackout in the history of the United States know what it's all about. But even prior to the Big Blackout, there were smaller ones and various brownouts—that is, periods when voltage was reduced enough to cause lights to dim and TVs to go haywire.* Did the East Coast blackout occur because New Yorkers were using too much electricity? Have brownouts occurred because people in various sectors of the nation are overconsuming scarce energy? In a way, yes. Obviously, brownouts and blackouts only occur when excessive demands are made on a utility system. To understand why these excessive demands occur when they do, we need look no further than the way electricity is sold.

You are probably aware of the fact that utilities are generally called public utilities because they serve the

---

*One observer maintains that electricity voltage reductions are the machinations of labor-intensive massage parlors trying to put capital-intensive ones out of business.

public (I guess). They are regulated, not only by their state public service commissioners, but also by the Federal Power Commission. This regulation takes on a complicated but understandable form. Public utilities are generally allowed to make a normal rate of return or profit on the capital that has been invested in them. In other words, they get to set their prices so as to yield this normal profit. In this manner, they are presumably prevented from charging monopoly prices, and therefore from obtaining monopoly profits. Another way of regulating them is to allow them to charge a price which just covers their costs plus a normal profit. In any event, regulation has typically taken on a *fixed rate* nature. Utilities in the United States in general have not been allowed to charge different prices to the same customers at different times of the day or year. That means that when you turn on your air conditioner in New York on a balmy August afternoon when the temperature is 98 degrees and the humidity is 99.9 percent, you pay the same price per killowatt as you do when you turn on the bathroom light at 3 o'clock in the morning on a pleasant spring day. Now, does anyone have any incentive to conserve on the use of electricity during the peak periods when the system can get overloaded? Not so far as I can tell. Given the fixed rate structure of prices that electric utilities are allowed to charge, they have no choice but to increase capacity so as to prevent peak period demand from wiping them out and causing the system to shut down completely, like on the East Coast. Think about the costs imposed on all users of electricity in an area by the customer who puts the last straw on the camel's back. Immense, isn't it? Probably to be measured in millions of dollars.

The problem, then, is to figure out a way to avoid too much demand all at once. Now obviously we can't do it by identifying the customer who breaks the system's back, and even if we could, we're not about to charge him a few million dollars. But we do have an alternative, and one that is embarrassingly simple: Why not charge people a higher price for electricity when it's the scarcest? Otherwise stated, why not put a peak time surcharge on it? It can be done, technologically at least. And it's rational from an economic efficiency point of view. They've done it in France and it seems to work; we could try it in the U.S.

Some people maintain it won't work, though, because people won't respond to higher prices during hot days by turning down their air conditioners. Since nobody's ever tried it here, how can we be sure? Isn't it worth a try? It's certainly preferable to try something like that rather than to impose rationing or to continuously incur brownouts and blackouts during peak periods. It will also give utilities additional funds for expansion. And in fact, it seems like the only fair way to charge people. After all, those who use electricity during the peak times are the ones responsible for the continued expansion of generation capacity. Why shouldn't they be the ones to have to pay a surcharge, the proceeds from which can go to building additional capacity? A lot of times during the day and during the year, most electrical systems are not operating at full capacity, but they're being built in order to meet the peak demands, and those of you who continue to demand electricity during those critical periods are forcing utilities to ever expand.

Don't get the impression, however, that having a more complex pricing system for electricity is going to solve all our problems. It won't. What it will do is make the existing and future systems more efficient and prevent the necessity of turning voltages down merely because of excessive demands during particular times of the day or the night and during particular seasons. Further, we might not to have to expand capacity at anywhere near the rate that's being planned.

If it's so simple, you might be asking, why won't the regulators allow companies to do it? The reason, of course, is because the regulators would be embarrassed. They don't like to allow price rises that cause profits to increase for public utilities, because their mandate is to prevent monopoly profits from actually being reaped. But there is a way out if that's a big worry. The way out is to take the surcharges, put them in a trust fund, and allow the electric utilities to use them only for expansion. Alternatively, rates for offpeak use could be lowered; the "bad" guys will subsidize the "good" guys.

It's going to be a while, you can be sure, before electric utility regulators, or the Federal Power Commission, or both get around to changing their procedures. In large part, much of our energy problem can be laid squarely on the backs of these regulators. One of the most effective ways man has invented to get people to not use so much of a scarce resource is by making it hurt more to use it. How? Simply by raising the price. Utility regulators have been used to falling electricity rates for such a long time that they were caught off guard when inflation took off in the latter sixties. What had happened until then is that the electric utility industry had taken advantage of newer technologies, economics of scale, and so on, to such an extent that average electricity prices fell over a long, long period. In the latter part of the 1960s, however, inflation increased. The prices of the inputs used to generate and distribute electricity started going up also. In particular, the capital expenses—that is, the costs of building new generating capacity—rose dramatically.

Consequently, electric companies started asking for, of all things, rate increases. Regulators didn't know what to do. They had been the heroes for a long, long time, reigning over an era of falling rates; suddenly they were about to become the villains in an inflationary plot to squelch the consumer. They resisted, then, and they are still resisting. Regulatory lag has always been long. But now it's becoming disasterous. What does this mean? It means that by the time regulators okay a rate increase, the cost of providing the service has gone up even more. Of course, eventually everything will probably work itself out, but why do we have to wait? Electric utilities could reduce the amount of electricity consumed dramatically by charging people the true value of the energy they're getting. What is the true value? It's what has to be given up to provide that energy. If to expand the system in order to increase electricity generation it's going to cost the company three times the current price it's charging, then the cost of that additional electricity to the consumer should probably be considerably higher than it is.

Unfortunately, regulators will never allow this. They will never allow electric utilities to charge the full, long-run (incremental) costs for electricity. Why? For the same reason that they won't allow utilities to charge customers more during peak periods of demand. Profits would go up too high and it would be embarrassing. But there's a way out of this, the same one suggested before. Electric utilities could be forced to put any excess profits into a trust fund. Or they could be taxed away. What's important is that you and I be forced to face the true cost of our actions. If that means paying a higher price for electricity during peak use periods, so be it. If that means that you and I ultimately are going to have to pay the full cost of expanding electric generating facilities, so be it. If it also means that we have to pay for the full cost of any environmental damage caused in providing us with that additional electricity, so be it. This issue is itself part of the current problem, and one sufficiently important to treat in greater detail later on. Note that when we pay these higher prices, we must give up consuming something else; hence, we indirectly release the resources needed to produce what we buy.

Utility regulation has certainly been lax over the past few years. But according to some economists, that's what we should expect. Take the electric utility industry itself and its regulators. Academic studies of electric utility regulation have yielded surprising conclusions. One is that the individual utility system really doesn't have any monopoly power in the first place because it faces competition from other energy sources. It also faces competition from other utility systems to which in the long run its industrial (and therefore many of its residential) users may move. Additionally, one study showed that in almost all cases, a regulatory body would be incapable of forcing an electric utility to operate at a specified combination of output, price, and cost because it's impossible to regulate all the various quality aspects of electricity sales. In an editorial comment prefacing a study with these conclusions, economist P.M. MacAvoy of MIT notes that these conclusions, in spite of many critical comments, remain relatively secure. But these conclusions are no different than those reached by other economists studying other regulatory bodies. Regulation of anything is at best difficult, and at worst impossible. The egregious effects of socially inappropriate regulation can sometimes be felt nationwide. Take the example of the Federal Power Commission. It controls interstate natural gas sales. What it has done for so many years now is keep the price of natural gas so low that it encouraged nonconservation in the consumption of that gas and discouraged exploration for any more. After all, it's only human nature for us to use more of that which is cheaper. And it's only businessmen's nature to invest less capital in less profitable endeavors.

As we shall see, the continued "shortage" of natural gas has been universally recognized as a problem of a too low price set by the Federal Power Commission. At one and the same time, this artificially low price has created a shortage and given no incentive for the shortage to disappear over time. It's not surprising that utilities, schools, and manufacturers became more dependent on oil and less dependent on natural gas as the "shortage" problem became ever more serious. Hence, the possibility of disruption due to any oil cutoff with no alternatives available was increased, but more on that later.

In spite of the fact that even the Sierra Club has come out for a rise in the price of electricity, many are still convinced that what we really have to do to solve the electricity problem at least, and more generally, the energy crisis, is to change our life styles. We've become too energy dependent, so let's get back to the simple life.

CHAPTER 5

The New Puritanism

You're probably pretty certain that there is much waste of electricity in these United States. Most of us know that there are indeed numerous frivolous uses of that scarce resource. A lot of people have suggested that we cut out those frivolous uses. Okay, let's do it. What do you think will happen? Nothing (or almost nothing). Impossible you say. People are buying so many needless electric gadgets that if they stopped using them, we probably wouldn't have an energy shortage. You might be right, of course, but you'd have to establish a very exaggerated definition of frivolous to validate your conclusion. Let's look at some numbers, boring though they may be. Let's say that everybody in the United States—man, woman, and child—has an electric toothbrush and uses it three times a day. We decide, however, that this is a frivolous use of energy and all the electric toothbrushes go silent. Do you know what that would do to reduce the total amount of electricity consumed? It would reduce it by a tremendous 6/10,000ths of 1 percent. Surprising, isn't it? Well, read on.

If you totaled all of the "frivolous" uses of energy, you would find that the percentage of the total used is trivial. Look at the accompanying tables. Here you see uses of energy and their growth rates in the domestic economy from 1960 to 1968, the period for which the latest figures are available. Notice in Table 3 that the largest single determinant of the total *rate* of growth was transportation. What about air conditioning? A mere 1.7 percent. What about residential cooking on those energy hungry gas and electric ovens? A mere 0.5 percent of the total growth. Obviously, even if we could change our life styles over night and eliminate all frivolous uses of electricity, we wouldn't change the energy picture very much.

Perhaps more disturbing is the tendency for so many people to *want* the energy crisis. Why? Because it's making us go back to old values, ones we used to have. There are even magazine articles now entitled "Learning to Love the Energy Crisis." Let's look at some of the good old things we used to have before we became energy pigs.

In the good old days, people used to sit on their front porches and rock during the summer, saying "Howdy" to all passers-by. But they don't do that any more. Why? Because they're inside being air conditioned. Looking at the possibility of a permanent reduction in speed limits on major highways, observers point out the huge benefits in changing life styles. After all, if we all drive at 50, life's pace will slow down, making each driver coming on and off the expressway easier to deal with. He'll become more human, more warm (particularly without air conditioning in his car). If in fact the energy crisis continues indefinitely, walking may come back into style. Bicycles already have. The residential commercial centers will have to centralize so that people can get to them more easily without taking a car. Many maintain that the threat of an energy crisis has already (and perhaps permanently) caused people

Table 2
USES OF ENERGY IN THE DOMESTIC ECONOMY[1]

	Percent of Total
Transportation[2]	24.9%
Process steam[3] (industrial)	16.7
Direct heat[3] (industrial)	11.5
Space heating (residential)	11.0
Electric drive (industrial)	7.9
Space heating (commercial)	6.9
Feedstocks, raw materials (commercial, industrial, transportation)	5.5
Water heating (residential)	2.9
Air conditioning (commercial)	1.8
Lighting (residential, commercial)	1.5
Electrolytic processes (industrial)	1.2
Cooking (residential)	1.1
Refrigeration (residential)	1.1
Water heating (commercial)	1.1
Refrigeration (commercial)	1.1
Air conditioning (residential)	0.7
Cooking (commercial)	0.2
Other (includes clothes drying and other uses)	2.9
Total	100.0%

[1] Based on 1968 data. Later data are not available.

[2] Fuel; excludes lubes and greases.

[3] Includes some use for space heating, probably enough to bring total space heating to about 20 percent.

Source: Office of Science and Technology, Executive Office of the President, *Patterns of Energy Consumption in the United States.* Washington, D.C.: U.S. Government Printing Office, January 1972, pp. 6-7.

to turn their thermostats down to where they "should have been anyway." People will learn to live with less light, and perhaps go back to sitting around a fireplace. Anyway, wearing heavy sweaters wasn't all that bad, and all the

Table 3

GROWTH IN THE USES OF ENERGY IN THE DOMESTIC ECONOMY

	Annual Rate of Growth 1960–1968 (1)	*Percent of Total Growth 1960–1968* (2)
Transportation[1]	4.1%	23.9%
Process steam[2] (industrial)	3.6	14.2
Direct heat[2] (industrial)	2.8	7.9
Space heating (residential)	4.1	10.5
Electric drive (industrial)	5.3	9.3
Space heating (commercial)	3.8	6.1
Feedstocks, raw materials (commercial, industrial, transportation)	5.1	6.2
Water heating (residential)	5.2	3.3
Air conditioning (commercial)	8.6	3.1
Electrolytic processes (industrial)	4.8	1.3
Cooking (residential)	1.7	0.5
Refrigeration (residential)	8.2	1.8
Water heating (commercial)	2.3	0.6
Refrigeration (commercial)	2.9	0.8
Air conditioning (residential)	15.6	1.7
Cooking (commercial)	4.5	0.2
Other (includes clothes drying, lighting and other uses)	10.9	8.6
Total	4.3%	100.0%

[1] Fuel; excludes lubes and greases.
[2] Includes some use for space heating.

Source: Office of Science and Technology, Executive Office of the President, *Patterns of Energy Consumption in the United States.* Washington, D.C.: U.S. Government Printing Office, January 1972, p. 6.

extra effort we might have to expend to make up for the energy deficit might help us lose some weight. Wouldn't that be great?

Of course, you can argue all of these things 'till you're blue in the face and nothing will ever be proven. What I would like to point out is merely that different people have different values. It was disturbing indeed to see those with more puritanical, less consumption-oriented values try to use an energy crisis to impose themselves on every-one else. To be sure, a number of things that all of us do involve social costs that we aren't forced to pay. But doesn't that mean that we should be forced to pay those social costs and then still be allowed to decide what we want to do? Not so, according to the new puritans. They know what's good for you. What's good for you is the good, simple life in a slightly chilly house in the winter, in a hotter house in the summer, on your feet instead of in your car, and so on. I must admit that I personally do not have the nerve to tell you how to live. I can say that perhaps you ought to pay for the pollution your car is causing and all the congestion you are creating because I suffer from that pollution and that congestion. I might be able to say I think you should be charged the full social costs of the electricity you're using because otherwise I will have to pay the difference. But I just can't get myself into a frame of mind that permits me to tell you how to run your life. One man's Nixon may be another's McGov-ern. It's certainly not up to me to decide.

We've seen that the new puritanism took over from the very beginning of the energy crisis and manifested itself as soon as government officials were allowed to make rules and regulations designed to conserve energy. All that was essential was to be kept; all that was frivolous to be jettisoned. Now you know as well as I do that the human creature has an infinite capacity to figure out how to make himself better off, no matter what the situation. Hence, even the most stringent attempts at regulating his life style would be and have been met by persistent weaseling on the part of every individual. This might be viewed as the era of weaseling your way to where you want to be even if it takes *more* energy to do it. Of course, that is called unpatriotic, at least according to those who make rules in an attempt to alter your life style. And of course many, at least for a short period of time, may voluntarily agree to turn their thermostats down, to drive less, or to turn off their lights, and to get ready to accept even worse. But under any circumstances, how long could volunteerism last when it means doing what you don't want to do just for the sake of the country? After all, the only official war we've been fighting for the last couple of years is against inflation. And since we've been about as successful there as we were in Vietnam, patriotism hasn't been running at the highest possible level.

A point that is often overlooked is that life styles have been changing all along in response to changing relative availabilities of different resources. If electricity is indeed less available today than in the past, its price can reflect that painful fact of life. If the price goes up sufficiently, you won't need moral philosophy to exhort us (nay, force us) to change our life styles. We will do it voluntarily (and undramatically, though the final outcome may be dramatic indeed).

CHAPTER 6

Energy Pigs
Versus our Grandchildren

According to Stewart Udall, Americans are energy pigs operating on some misguided assumption that the quantity of energy is limitless. Whether that's the way people have thought or still think is probably irrelevant to any analysis of the energy crisis. What we do have to decide, however, is whether we are conserving energy in a correct manner so as not to cheat future generations. Remember, now, when we talk about energy, we're talking about all sources. Today we get 17 percent from coal, 44 percent from oil, 32 percent from natural gas, 3 percent from nuclear power plants, and 4 percent from hydro sources. We also get a little bit from geothermal heat out of steam, hot water, and hot rock, and could at some point tap solar radiation, wind power, sea thermal gradients, photosynthesis, organic wastes and tidal energy. In any event, the resources we are talking about are for all practical purposes nonrenewable, unlike, for example, trees. Even the breeder technology for nuclear fission has a limit. Breeder reactors don't actually create more fuel; they make existing fuel usable not unlike the way a burning fire dries out wet logs to make them usable later on. And of course there is the possibility of nuclear fusion in the future.

Americans use a prodigous amount of energy, perhaps accounting for one-third of the world's consumption. The rate at which the United States uses energy has, of course, been growing, even doubling in the past twenty years. When will the widow's cruse run out? We saw in previous chapters that it is impossible to estimate oil reserves because they keep growing, being greater now than they were thirty-five years ago. If this is the case, how do we figure out a conservation program? In fact, is there a need for a conservation program, and, if so, will it solve our energy problems?

First of all, let's try to get an operationally meaningful definition of conservation. The first head of the U.S. Forest Service, Gifford Pinchot, felt that "conservation means the greatest good for the greatest numbers, and that for the longest time." Now should this be our *modis operandi* for conserving energy resources? Well, not if you think about it because it doesn't make sense.

We know that at any moment in time the total amount of resources in the United States (or, for that matter, in the world) is fixed. Therefore, whenever you use a resource, nobody else can use it. Whatever other people use, you cannot use.* This makes it quite difficult to talk about the greatest good for the greatest number and is a good example of what economists refer to as erroneous and impossible double maximization. It would be like saying you want the best for the least. Either you seek the highest quality product you can buy for a given price or for a given quality you seek out the lowest priced brand. The same holds for conservation. In sum, it is impossible

---

*There are exceptions and these are called public goods.

to have the greatest good for the greatest number because what one person has, another person doesn't have.

Now consider the clause "and that for the longest time." What does this mean? What could it possibly lead to in terms of the use of energy resources? Doesn't it imply that no resources should be used at all today and forever after? That, of course, is how we use our energy resources for the longest time—by never using them up at all! We can keep all the coal in the ground from now to eternity by never taking any out. We can keep all the oil in the ground from now to eternity by never putting another well in, and by closing up all the ones we have. But does conservation in fact really mean that we should limit the amount of energy resources we use so that they will last the longest time? If so, we should stop consuming completely today. Then our grandchildren and their grandchildren and their grandchildren will inherit the largest amount of natural resources.

I don't think that is what anybody really has in mind. Perhaps another definition of conservation can be found, one that will give us a rational objective standard by which to judge current activities involving energy resources.

Let's look at the simple example of an acre of land which has some trees on it. Suppose you are the owner of that land. How should you decide whether to cut the trees or let them grow? If you decide to cut the trees, then you have to determine when you cut them and how many. Should you cut one tree, two trees, or all the trees?

Let's make the problem simple and assume that the trees are located in an area that no one ever sees. We will assume you get no pleasure from the mere fact of owning trees. You are a wealth maximizer and look only at the monetary return to the piece of property that you own. If you wanted to maximize wealth, you would decide how to use your trees by looking at how profitable it would be to either cut them or let them grow. That's a hard decision but really no different from the decisions facing any property owner. He must decide the optimal use of his resource. With natural resources, this also involves the optimal *timing* of the use of the resources.

If you thought you could build a road to your stand of trees and then charge campers a certain amount of money to use the area, you would consider this as an alternative way to use your resource. You could also cut down all the trees today, sell them on the open market, and receive a certain price per tree. If you waited another year, you could sell them on the open market and you'd perhaps receive a different price. Since the trees would have grown during that time, there would be more board feet of lumber to sell. Obviously, if you thought that the price was going to rise in the future and the trees were going to grow bigger, you might want to wait to cut them. But obviously you shouldn't wait forever. At some point you will maximize your net wealth position by cutting the trees or, if camping becomes very lucrative, by making your tree stand into a private campground. The point is that you must compare the benefits from not cutting trees with the costs of not cutting trees. The available benefits of not cutting at all stem from the fact that the area could be used as a campground. Moreover, if you do not cut, you might get a higher price for them in the future.

Your costs are the "opportunity" costs of not cutting the trees and not selling them for what you could get. If, for example, you could sell them for $1 million this year and invest that money in a comparatively risk-free government bond which yielded a 6 percent rate of return, the opportunity cost of not cutting the trees is going to be equal to 6 percent of $1 million, or $60,000. The combined benefit of not cutting the trees—that is, the benefit of a potential higher price in the future with bigger trees to sell—must at least equal the $60,000. Otherwise, you would cut the trees right away. (You also have the alternative of cutting now and then replanting. You might want to sell the timberland with small young trees on it.)

In order to maximize the value of a piece of property that has natural resources on it, you should time your use of those resources so as to maximize the *discounted* value of the resources. Let's discuss the concept of discounting. If you get a dollar today, it's worth a dollar; but if you get a dollar one year from now, it is not worth $1 in today's terms. It is worth less. You must discount tomorrow's dollar back to today to find out what it is really worth to you. After all, today's dollars could be put in a savings and loan association to earn interest. If somebody said you had to pay them one dollar a year from now, you might be able to put 95¢ in the bank and earn interest so that in one year, you would be able to pay the dollar. Thus, *costs which are borne in the future are less of a burden than those which must be paid today.*

The same is true of benefits. In this particular case, the benefits will be the income received from cutting the timber. Money that is forthcoming a year from now will be worth less than money today. Even if you didn't want to invest the money you have today, you would be better off having it today than in the future because you have the opportunity to invest it or spend it during the interim. *Benefits are worth less the further away they are in the future.* If you have an acre of trees, you will estimate how much money you will receive for each time profile of cutting them. (You could sell the land and trees, too.) As mentioned before, it may turn out that you should never cut them if, in fact, the money you can make from turning the acre into a private campground exceeds the money you can make from cutting the trees. That, in fact, has happened in some areas of this country. As public campgrounds (for which users are usually charged a below market-clearing price) become more and more crowded, private campgrounds become more attractive to individuals and, therefore, more and more private campgrounds have sprung up throughout the United States. There was a 15 percent increase in such campgrounds from 1970 to 1971.

Conservation now takes on a very definite meaning. The definition we shall use will be that *conservation means the optimal timing of the use of our fixed amount of resources.* What does optimal timing involve? This merely means utilizing resources in such a way that the value today of the streams of (net) benefits from those resources is greatest. We can apply this definition to many of the problems of conserving our natural resources. Let's do that now.

There is much concern about using up all of the natural gas under this earth. There's also much concern about using up all of the iron ore, coal, oil, or any of the other minerals and resources that are found in the earth which cannot be renewed (or can only renew themselves very slowly). This is not the case, of course, with trees: we can always plant more trees. But lots of resources cannot be renewed. Many conservationists believe that because they cannot be renewed, their use should be limited. Using our newly found definition of conservation, we can agree that the use of such resources should indeed be limited, but not to the degree of never using them. After all, if the coal in the earth is never used, the present value of that coal will be zero. We'll never obtain any benefits from it. Neither will our grandchildren nor their grandchildren because they will never be able to use it to furnish energy. If it will never yield a benefit in the future, then the value today of that coal is zero. The question really is: how fast should we use our coal? How fast should we use our natural gas? Inevitably, we will eventually run out of many of our natural resources if we consume them at some constant rate forever. Any finite use of resources will eventually deplete nonrenewable resources unless their quantity is infinite. The only thing that holds true is that the slower we use them, the longer they will last. But how do we decide the rate at which we should actually use these resources?

Again, we can go back to a wealth-maximizing situation. Now we will want to assume that it is the wealth of the entire world that is important. Here we can use our same criterion. The value from nonrenewable resources is maximized if they are used at different periods of time so that the net present value of these resources is highest. You might immediately scream "bloody murder" at this criterion, for it leads to an eventual depletion of the kinds of resources with which you are familiar. Let's again consider the case of natural gas. It is true that we may eventually run out of natural gas if we continue using it. First of all, we will not continue using it at its same rate if the Federal Power Commission allows the price to rise. As the price of natural gas becomes higher, which it will as it becomes scarcer, people will seek less expensive alternatives. This is one key to understanding why there is a limit to how much of any natural resource will be used. After some point, the resource becomes so expensive that nobody uses it any more. In fact, we may never run out of natural gas because it will become prohibitively expensive to take it out of the ground. People will use substitutes.

The use of substitutes is another key to understanding why it might be better to use up some of our natural resources rather than limit their use today. If we do not use natural gas, for example, we will use oil, coal, or some other form of energy. If we restrict the production and consumption of any one of our natural resources, we can be sure that some others will be used more intensively or other substitutes will be developed. That means that they will be used up faster than otherwise. *It is impossible to conserve everything because that means that we would have to cease to exist.* It is also somewhat naive to talk in terms of conserving only one or a selected few natural resources because then other resources will be used up more quickly. If in fact we want to maximize the benefits from our available resources, we would be wise to use up the cheapest ones first and then go on to the more inaccessible and less readily available ones. This can perhaps be best illustrated by an example.

Assume that the government has a million dollars to invest in the economy. What if the government decides to invest the million dollars in a project that yields a rate of return of 5 percent and the rate of return in the private (nongovernmental) sector is 10 percent? Future generations will *not* be better off because of the government investment. They would inherit a larger capital stock—that is, more wealth—if the government had not used the million dollars at all, which it would have gotten from the private sector in the first place, had instead allowed the private sector to use it in private investment where it would yield a rate of return of 10 percent. By the time future generations arrived, they would have the million dollars compounded at 10 percent rather than at 5 percent. The same goes for the use of natural resources.

If we decide to use a combination of natural resources that has a higher cost than some other combination, we will be cheating future generations, not helping them out. It may be that if we decide to use less natural gas and more oil, for example, the wealth that future generations will inherit will be less than it would be otherwise. We will be doing future generations a disfavor by being "conservationist-minded" (unless, of course, we decide to use less of *all* energy sources). Admittedly, this is a hard concept to accept because it does mean allowing nonrenewable resources to be depleted if that is in fact the cheapest way to provide the consumption and investment that the present generation wishes to engage in. But acting in any other way would leave future generations worse off, contrary to the notion of most conservationists. Conservation cannot mean limiting the use of our resources; it has to mean maximizing the benefits from our limited resources.

A common argument is that this essentially profit motive oriented scheme overlooks the welfare of future generations; we deplete the oil, for example, too fast because we don't care whether the next generation is well off. But look at it this way: First, the well being of future generations largely depends on our *saving* behavior, and conservation may take place in the absence of any real savings. Second, even if I am ninety years old, I intensely care for future generations because the present value of my oil wells, which determines my immediate consumption, depends on rationing the oil output among individuals that will stay alive *after* I am gone.

One thing that we have almost completely ignored up till now involves the pollution problems inherent in the use of energy; that is what we turn to next.

CHAPTER 7

Paying for Energy Pollution

Until very recently we have been able to use energy without taking account of the cost that use imposed on our deteriorating environment. Oil spills in the ocean increased, smog in the air thickened, and our rivers became cesspools. The helter-skelter building of power plants was allowed to go unabated, no matter how ugly and destructive to the environment they were. But times have changed. We are no longer in an era when energy pollution is allowed to go unabated, and of course that fact has exacerbated the energy crisis. We have, through various means, increased our demands for energy sources to get the same level of BTUs. Our automobiles get poorer gas mileage because of smog control devices. (They pollute less per gallon of gas, but burn more gas.) Industry and electric utilities must burn scarcer, more expensive low sulfur fuel oil. Nuclear power plants have not been allowed to go "on stream" because of environmental problems.

The list goes on, but it all comes back to the same problem we are just now facing up to: we haven't directly been paying the full cost of our energy in the past. We are finally beginning to move a little closer to that goal. It is interesting to note that as soon as an energy crisis appeared, everybody started clamoring for a relaxation of pollution abatement standards in industry and for automobiles. You will see that this is not necessarily an appropriate way to solve the energy problem. For if we are now reaching a more nearly optimal relationship between costs of energy and prices charged, then jettisoning pollution controls will get us right back to where we started—right back to an excessive rate of pollution production.

Let's first try to figure out why we have had too much pollution to begin with, whether it be from automobile engine exhaust fumes, electric utility steam generators, or oil tanker ocean spills. We have to determine the reason why some economic agents—i.e., the polluters—can do harm to our environment without paying the consequences. After all, no production process known to man is waste-free.

Look at it this way. When a businessman has to pay wages to workers, he knows exactly what his labor costs are. When he has to buy materials or build a plant, he knows quite well what it will cost him. When an individual has to pay for fixing his car, or pay for a pair of shoes, or for a theater ticket, he knows exactly what his cost will be. These very explicit costs are what we term *private costs*. Private costs are those borne solely by the individuals who incur them. They are internal in the sense that the firm or household must explicitly take account of them.

Note that we all "pollute" our houses, our clothes, etc., so pollution is not unique to external effects; it is a problem only when it is not internalized, as in the above pollution examples. It is also internalized in, say, movie theaters, not by polluters cleaning up their own mess, but by their paying high enough entry prices to cover costs that include cleaning.

Consider now the situation where a businessman can dump the waste products from his production process into a nearby river. Or what about instances where an individual can litter a public park or beach? Obviously a cost is involved in these actions. When the businessman pollutes the water, people downstream suffer the consequences. They drink the polluted water and swim and bathe in it. They're also unable to catch as many fish as before because of the pollution. In the case of littering, the people who bear the costs are those who come along after our litterer has cluttered that part of the beach. The scenery will certainly be less attractive. We see that the cost of these actions are borne by people other than those who commit the actions. That is to say, the creator of the cost is not the bearer. The costs are not internalized; they are *external*. When we add external costs to internal or private costs, we come up with *social costs*. They are called social costs because it is society in general which bears the costs and not just the individuals who create them. Pollution problems and, indeed, all problems pertaining to the environment may be viewed as situations where social costs are different than private costs. Since some economic agents don't pay the full social costs of their actions, but rather only the smaller private costs, their actions are said to be socially excessive.

To cite an example, let's ask ourselves why the air in cities is so polluted from automobile exhaust fumes. When automobile drivers step into their cars, they bear only the private costs of driving. That is, they must pay for the gas, maintenance, depreciation, and insurance on their automobiles. However, they cause an additional cost—that of air pollution—which they are not forced to take account of when they make the decision to drive. The air pollution created by automobile exhaust is a social cost which, as yet, individuals do not bear directly. The social cost of driving includes all the private costs plus the cost of air pollution, noise pollution, congestion, etc., which society bears. Decisions that are made on the basis of private costs will only lead to too much automobile driving or, alternatively, to too little money spent, for example, on the reduction of automobile pollution.

We can see here an "easy" method of reducing the amount of pollution and environmental degradation that now exists. Somehow the signals in the economy must be changed so that decision makers will take into account all of the costs of their actions. In the case of automobile pollution, we might want to devise some method whereby motorists were taxed according to the amount of pollution they caused. In the case of a firm, we might want to devise some system whereby businessmen were charged (i.e., taxed) according to the amount of pollution they were responsible for. In this manner, they would have an incentive to install pollution abatement equipment.

When you think about it, however, it may not be appropriate to levy a uniform tax according to physical quantities of pollution. After all, we're talking about *social* costs. Such costs are not necessarily the same everywhere in the United States for the same action. If you drive your smelly, belching car in the middle of the Mohave Desert, you will probably inflict your damage on scorpions only, and they don't have much political pull. The natural cleansing action of the large body of air around you will eliminate the pollution you generate to such an extent that it creates no economical harm. If a businessman pollutes the water in a lake that is used by no one except him and the lake is, in fact, inaccessible to everyone except him, the economic damages he creates by polluting may be negligible and are certainly internalized.

Essentially, we must establish the size of the economic damages rather than the size of the physical amount of pollution. A polluting electric steam-generating plant in New York City will cause much more damage than the same plant in, say, Nowhere, Montana. This is so because the concentration of people in New York City is much higher than in Nowhere. There are already innumerable demands on the air in New York City, so that the pollution from smokestacks will not naturally be cleansed away. There are millions of people who will breathe that smelly air and thereby incur the costs of sore throats, emphysema, and even early death. There are many, many buildings which will become dirtier faster because of the pollution, and many more cars and clothes will also become much dirtier. The list goes on and on, but it should be obvious that a given quantity of pollution will cause more harm in concentrated urban environments than it will in less dense rural environments. If we wish to establish some form of taxation that could align social costs with private costs and could force people to internalize externalities, we would somehow have to come up with a devise for measuring economic costs instead of physical quantities.

Now let's find out why there will be a divergence between social costs and private costs. Why do certain situations create externalities, while others do not? For example, consider some of the things you own. Suppose you own a bicycle. If someone comes along and somehow alters it unfavorably by slashing the tire or bending the spokes, you can, in principle, press criminal charges or at least civil charges and recover damages. The damages you recover would at least be equal to the reduction in the market value of your bike. The same goes for a car, if you own one. Anyone damaging your car is liable for those damages. The courts will uphold your right to compensation.

What if you live next to a stinky steel factory? The air around you—which is something that you have to use—is damaged. You are also damaged by breathing it. However, you do not necessarily have any grounds for stopping the air pollution or for obtaining compensation for the destruction of the air around you. This is so because you do not have rights to the air surrounding you, nor does

anyone else. Air happens to be a common property resource. Herein lies the crux of the problem: whenever
property rights are undefined or nonexistent, social costs
may be different than private costs, particularly in the
situations we will outline below. This is as you would
expect. When no one owns a particular resource, people do
not have an incentive to consider their particular despoilia-
tion of that resource. In fact, a person would be foolish to
do so. If one person decides not to pollute the air, there
will be no general effect on the total level of pollution and
so he is no better off by his own actions. If one person
decides not to pollute the ocean, there will still be the
same general amount of ocean pollution, provided of
course that the individual is but a small part of the total
number of polluters.

When property rights are in existence, individuals have
legal recourse to any damages sustained through the misuse
of their property. When property rights are well defined,
the use of property—that is, the use of resources—will
generally involve contracting between the owners of those
resources. If you owned any land, you might contract with
another person so that he could use your land for, say,
raising cows.* The contract would most likely be written
up in the form of a rental agreement. We can probably
predict that whenever contracting becomes exceedingly
expensive or difficult, social and private costs will diverge.
Whenever contracting is relatively costless, social costs and
private costs will end up being one and the same thing. In
fact, this is why externalities are only problems in certain
areas of activity in our society. We don't worry about
social and private costs with the majority of all the activities that go on in our economy because almost all of what

---

*Others might contract with you *not* to allow smelly cows on
your land.

goes on involves contracting among individuals and the transference of property rights.

Instead of attempting to tax polluters in proportion to the economic damages caused by their pollution, we could define property rights more precisely so that contracting would have to take place. For example, we might want to make factories liable for the pollution that they create. When we do that, we are implicitly vesting property rights in the common property resources of water and air surrounding the factories. The individuals living there will implicitly be the owners of the air and water if they get the proceeds from the tax. The factory will therefore be liable for its using the water and air in a manner which imposes costs on others.

In a sense, this is not really "fair." After all, a common property resource is, by definition, owned by everyone. We would be arbitrary in assigning property rights in a common property resource to the homeowners, just as we would be arbitrary in assigning the property rights to the factory. But, due to the fact that it is easier to make the individual factory owner pay, we still might want to go ahead with this arbitrary assignment of property rights. In essence, the government will have to act in behalf of the homeowners when dealing with the polluting factory. The government will somehow have to come up with the value of the economic damages that the factory's pollution is causing and require that the factory make due compensation or install pollution abatement equipment. The compensation would have to be distributed to the homeowners in a manner that reflected the economic cost sustained by each of them. That too, of course, is a difficult problem. It might be simpler to use the "bribe" money to clean up some of the pollution caused by the factory instead of trying to compensate the losers (the individual homeowners). *Note here that the optimal level of pollution is not zero.* The optimal level is that point where the social benefits of further reducing pollution just equal the social costs of doing so. In other words, if contracting were costless, the parties to the contract would have agreed to a nonzero level of pollution by which the polluter would compensate the damaged one.

We all seem to think that the problem of pollution is something new to the sixties and seventies, but this is not the case. London has had smog for well over a century because its densely distributed inhabitants burned soft coal. Los Angeles has been smog-filled for many, many years, and Pittsburgh used to be dark during the day in some sections of the city. In fact, we know there's always been some pollution because it is impossible to produce anything without waste by-products. However, many observers feel that in the past the natural cleansing action of the earth's waters and air seemed to be able to cope with the waste products that man created. According to these same people, until the last 10 to 20 years the level of pollution in many parts of the United States was apparently not over the level that could be tolerated by the vast absorptive capacities of water and of air.

It seems that this is no longer the case. Population increased by 24 million between 1960 and 1970, and it is projected to increase by the same amount during this decade. Additionally, each of us now consumes more, and in so doing, produces more pollution. There has also been an increased concentration of people in urban areas. This has been a trend that was established in the very beginnings of our country. Right now, over half of the population is crowded into 1 percent of our land, and two-thirds crowd themselves onto less than 10 percent of the land. In these urban environments, there are many manufacturing plants, power plants, and transportation facilities which are so highly concentrated that the natural environment can no longer absorb our waste products.

Even though the air and water pollution problem seems

to be getting worse, we should remember that cities have always been places of pollution concentration. Before there was the automobile, horses made city streets unusable for foot traffic except for those people wearing very high-topped boots. The burning of coal with high sulfur content polluted the air in London for many, many years until that particular type of coal was banned. Believe it or not, the quantity of air pollution in London is lower today than it was 100 years ago. Some economic historians contend that the quality of life in our crowded cities is not necessarily lower today than it was in years past, but we will not attempt to argue this controversial point. The fact remains that we have levels of pollution which many of us believe to be too high.

Consider the specific case of air pollution. The largest physical quantity of air pollution consists of carbon monoxide, of which over 60 percent is generated by transportation vehicles: cars, buses, planes, and so on. We are showered with 30 million tons of particulates every year. Particulates are things you can see: bits of ash, carbon, oil, grease, and metallic substances. In some cities the level of particulates in the air is high enough to cause citizens to believe the cant: "We don't trust any air we can't see."

Motor vehicles are a prime source of air pollution, and there are over 100 million vehicles on the road today. Internal combustion, gasoline-powered cars and buses also emit unburned hydrocarbons, lead compounds, nitrogen oxides, carbon monoxide, compounds of phosphorus, lead, and additional unburned organic compounds. Why haven't manufacturers developed a cleaner burning engine so that auto exhaust fumes do not choke our precious air? Why don't motorists pay heed to the pollution problem they are causing?

The answers have already been given. Until very recently, auto manufacturers and motorists were not forced to pay the costs they imposed on the rest of society by stinking up our air. Anybody who got into his car could ignore the pollution problem he was adding to. In any event, his single contribution remains, for all practical purposes, negligible. If he decides not to drive or to use an engine which emits no pollution, the total quantity of pollution will remain the same because he is such a small part of the total problem. Air in this particular case is a common property resource; everybody seems to want to use it in the manner that suits him best. The social cost of driving includes the air pollution caused by internal combustion engines. However, the private cost of driving does not, because nobody has to take account of what his exhaust fumes do to society.

Now things have changed. Air is still a common property resource, but the federal and state governments have stepped in to enforce emission control regulations. The federal government, for example, has set specific standards on the level of pollutants which can be emitted from any car's exhaust. These standards apply, however, only to new cars and it is quite obvious that they will not eliminate the problem completely because of all the older cars on the road. Moreover, unless there is some system whereby cars are checked periodically to make sure that their engines have been tuned properly and to make sure that their exhaust control systems have not been disconnected, we will probably not drastically alter the level of air pollution caused by vehicles. This problem is closely related to the property rights problem. If I owned the air, it would be costly to me to measure and police its use. That is why it is in the public domain. The new attempts to regulate the use of air have the same inherent problem of measurement and policing. So in general, most pollution problems are unlikely to be solved unless the solution itself is draconic—i.e., very costly.

The development of no-lead fuel created on potential way to eliminate some forms of air pollution from automobiles. The lead or ethyl in high-octane gasolines for high compression engines contributes substantially to air pollution. Therefore, it has been suggested that the lead content of gasoline be taxed. This particular method of pollution control was dropped in favor of requiring all cars to be built with engines that could run acceptably on low-octane, no-lead fuel. (These engines would have low compression ratios.) This particularly affected the performance of foreign imported cars which historically have relatively higher compression ratios than American engines. Here we find again that reduction of pollution is not costless.

People pay in reduced car performance in order to help eliminate pollution. When Mercedes-Benz came out with an eight-cylinder sports car, it turned out in some tests to be slower than the previous year's six-cylinder model. This happened because the new government standards requiring cars to be able to run on no-lead gas forced the compression ratio to be reduced so much that the car had a much less powerful engine. This is a good point to remember. Elimination of pollution will always involve a cost. In order to find out the entire cost, we must be careful to ferret out all of the ways individuals end up paying for pollution abatement.

What does the future hold for the automobile? Perhaps we will have electric cars in the future; but even here we will not eliminate all pollution. After all, an electric car's batteries have to be recharged with electricity, and that electricity has to be generated somewhere. When it is generated, the process of generation will itself cause pollution. In fact, electric power plants account for almost one-half of the emissions of sulfur oxides and one-fourth of the emissions of particulates in our air. Let's see what we must require from that sector of the economy in order to ease our pollution problem.

The generation of electricity has been doubling every ten years or less. At the beginning of the decade, over 16 billion kilowatt hours were generated. It is estimated that at current relative prices for electricity, by the year 2000 the demand will be six or seven times what it is today.

Right now most electricity is generated in steam power plants that burn fossil fuels. That is, some form of fuel such as oil, coal, or natural gas is burned to generate steam which runs large turbines that then create the electricity for the nation. In the process of burning fossil fuel—except, of course, for natural gas which burns with almost no pollution at all—sulfur oxides and particulate matters are injected into the air.

The government has stepped in to force electric power companies to account for the pollution they create when generating their product. The Clean Air Act was passed in 1970 and is the most stringent air quality measure that has ever been legislated. This act provides for setting up standards for stationary polluters, such as electric utilities. The standards will be based on what emission control capabilities are currently technologically feasible. Some states have gone further than the Clean Air Act by requiring that the sulfur content of the fuel burned must be 1 percent or less. The Nixon administration suggested a sulfur content tax but later changed its mind and opted for a tax on the sulfur emissions. This may be a much more economic way of controlling pollution. We really do not care what input goes into generating power, but we do care what the output is in terms of pollution content. A sulfur emissions tax will allow producers to find out the most efficient ways of eliminating pollution. This may be by burning lower sulfur content fuel; however, it may also turn out to be by installing pollution abatement equipment on the smokestack or something of that nature.

The generation of electricity has also caused problems with thermal pollution. Thermal pollution is thought to be "bad" by environmentalists. In fact, they brought a suit against the Baltimore Gas and Electric Company and stopped at least temporarily the construction of a nuclear power plant on Chesapeake Bay. The interveners pointed out that the National Environmental Policy Act of 1969 *required* that government agencies obtain environmental statements from companies and individuals seeking project clearance. In this case, the government agency which has to okay all the permits for building nuclear power plants is the Atomic Energy Commission (AEC). Until the Calvery Cliffs decision (a label taken from the area where the nuclear power plant was being built), the Atomic Energy Commission did not require very detailed environmental statements from electric utilities requesting nuclear power plant permits. Now the AEC must require utilities to go into a comprehensive and quantitative cost-benefit analysis for the power plant they propose to build.

Obviously, the costs that a utility has to consider are not only the private costs it will incur, but also the social costs it will force on society. The interveners in the Calvert Cliffs case maintained that thermal pollution would have killed many fish and therefore destroyed commercial and recreational fishing in that area. In order to determine whether the power plant should be built, some monetary value had to be placed on a fish kill.

The Calvert Cliffs decision has brought to the forefront the need to use comprehensive cost-benefit analysis when deciding to undertake a project that can seriously alter the environment. A nuclear power plant is such a project—and so is a highway, a fossil fuel steam generating plant, a dam, and many other government and private projects. Now it appears that there must be a reckoning of all costs and all benefits from proposed projects, and this reckoning must be, so far as is possible, quantitative. Today, it is no longer possible for even environmentalists to maintain that the status quo of the ecology is priceless and should not be altered. Rather, they too have to come up with a dollar figure; somehow they have to estimate the implicit value that people place on cold water in Chesapeake Bay and the results thereof. On the other hand, this also forces those seeking project clearance to do a quantitative assessment of the social costs and benefits involved. The benefits of relatively cheap nuclear power may be large indeed. In fact, when one considers the alternatives available for power generation, it may be that the costs of generating power in a nuclear power plant are less than the costs of generating power in a coal-fed or oil-fed steam generating plant. In order to find out if this is indeed the case, one would have to consider all possible economic damages that are incurred by each form of power generation. In the case of fossil fuel plants, there is air pollution and water pollution. In the case of nuclear power plants, there is thermal pollution and radiation pollution. Nuclear power plant builders maintain that the radiation surrounding a nuclear power plant is less than what we naturally incur in our daily lives. Of course, there is the possibility of a nuclear disaster if one of the power plants were to overheat or if something of that nature were to occur. The utilities companies maintain that the probability is so small as to be negligible, but if a disaster ever happened the consequences would be large indeed.

No matter what else happens, we will, because of the pollution abatement requirements now being imposed on the energy industry, see an increase in the relative price of energy. But apparently that is what we collectively desire. For that is the private price we have to pay for a cleaner environment, and if the decisions have been appropriately made, then there is little reason to give up the environmental ship whenever we have a temporary reduction in oil supplies.

The fact of the matter is, the crisis that everybody started to believe in during 1973 would not have been solved by scrapping environmental controls, nor by any of the myriad others offered and tried.

CHAPTER 8

How to Get a Crisis

Let's take a look at our first energy crisis, one that we experienced well over a hundred years ago. Then let's take a look at what happened during the last Middle East oil cutoff. (You may not even remember it.) And lastly, we'll look at the beef crisis we had. (You may not remember that, either.) After having taken the time to look back in history, we might be better able to understand what happened starting in the fall of 1973.

Before electricity was used to light our houses and our streets, the major source of artificial lighting, not only in Europe but in the U.S., was whale and sperm oil. At that time there were no good substitutes for these oils as sources of light, for petroleum had not yet been discovered in Pennsylvania. Hence, the entire world supply of light, except for the sun and moon, depended just about entirely on the whaling industry. We didn't have many sophisticated models, then, to tell us what the whale oil deficit was going to be. People knew it had to come about sooner or later. After all, the supply of whales couldn't keep pace with the increases in demand.

During the Civil War, the demand for whale oil increased

tremendously. Moreover, the supply fell abruptly, for there were war-caused disruptions in the production process. Whaling vessels were conscripted as freight ships. Additionally, Southern privateers captured or destroyed numerous whaling ships that had not been conscripted. The result—a 50 percent drop in the number of American whaling ships, a 60 percent drop in total tonnage. The crisis of artificial lighting fuel was obviously upon the nation.

But a funny thing happened. No crisis was ever talked about in the pubs or homes. What people talked about was the horrible rise in the price of whale oil. It cost so much more to read at night that some people decided it wasn't worth it. Sperm oil rose from 43¢ a gallon in 1823 to a whopping $2.55 a gallon in 1866. Similarly, whale oil's price rose from 23¢ in 1832 to $1.45 in 1865. These high prices of sperm and whale oil caused several things to happen, the first, the one we just mentioned; people started conserving whale oil because it was too expensive to waste. Another thing happened which is rarely remembered. As prices rose, the incentive for entrepreneurs to develop substitutes also rose. In Europe, gas that was distilled from coal suddenly became an economically feasible substitute, thus causing the quantity of whale oil demanded to drop off sharply. And now that petroleum had been discovered in Pennsylvania, it was just a matter of time until the high price of whale and sperm oil would induce profit-seeking businessmen to develop some sort of efficient refining process for crude oil.

So what happened was bound to happen. In 1867, kerosene became a cheap substitute for sperm and whale oil. By 1896, sperm oil was the cheapest it had been at any time, a mere 40¢ a gallon. A funny thing, though—very few people used it for lighting even at that price. Whale oil lamps were no more. The petroleum age was upon us.

We're obviously still living in that age, and it should

have come as no surprise that during the Middle East oil cut-off in 1967, a crisis was going to occur in the world energy market. You'll remember that during the 1967 Six Day War, the Suez Canal was completely cut off. The oil tanker fleet now had to go around Africa. So the same tanker capacity did not exist because of the increased length of the trip. And, within a short period of time, there was a massive reduction in the amount of oil flowing from the Persian Gulf countries. Fortunately for the United States, we were not importing very much during that year. But Europe was. We hastily met with our European partners and agreed to furnish them with needed oil. The effect, then, was the same as if we had been importing a lot of oil and it was cut off, as happened in 1973. We lost to Europe a significant fraction of our total crude oil.

But again nobody remembers a crisis! What people might remember is that the price of petroleum products rose after the Six Day War in 1967. As some observers point out, the oil companies took advantage of this excuse to raise prices, which they had been holding down in an implicit agreement with the government in exchange for the oil import restrictions referred to in Chapter 2. Another way of looking at it is that the reduction in supply with the same amount of oil demanded allowed U.S. companies to raise prices and still sell all that they had, since what they had was now reduced. After all, that's exactly what the OPEC countries started doing in 1973 as they reduced the quantity supplied to the rest of the world while raising prices. You can't sell the same amount at a higher price if nothing else changes. Hence, the only way to maintain a higher price is to restrict production. Everybody agrees that that's what the Arabs were doing starting in the fall of '73, so why shouldn't the same analysis hold when we essentially gave up part of our oil supply to Europe during the oil cut-off in '67?

These two episodes in the history of the United States

ought to make it easy to understand why nobody remembers the beef shortage that occurred in the summer of
1973. There was a while there when you would go into a
supermarket and find many of the beef bins empty. Now
how could that be? To understand how, you have to go
back to 1969. In that year, inflation was getting out of
hand and unemployment was rising. Unemployment continued relatively high through 1970; inflation kept up at a
positive pace, but peaked however in 1970 and started
going down hill. Then Phase I and the 90-day freeze were
proclaimed on August 15 a year later. Nixon's New Economic Policy was to be put to the test. Most observers now
look back with nostalgia on that first freeze, for when the
second one came around in June of '73, the true colors of
the particular set of controls Nixon had chosen were soon
seen. Some astute Nixonphiles contend that Phase 3½ was
deliberately set up by the president so as to fail in the most
disgraceful manner possible, thus teaching the American
public a lesson about the drawbacks of government intervention in the marketplace. The only truth to such wishful
thinking involves the first part of the story—Phase 3½ was
a disaster. Oddly enough, the freeze resulted in higher
prices for meat instead of steady or lower prices.

It all started back in March of '73. In response to
consumer complaints about increasingly high meat bills,
the government slapped a ceiling on meat prices. At that
time, red meat was selling at record levels and the meat
business was highly profitable. Nonetheless, overall inflation had presumably got out of hand because of a lax
Phase III and was taking its toll in feed prices. Soy bean
and feed grain costs went through the roof in response to
increased foreign as well as domestic demand. Feed lot
operators, who are the ones who buy the young animals to
fatten, promptly dropped their placements by over 10
percent in the second quarter of 1973 in response to high

production costs. Then the 60-day freeze came in June. Not only were feed lot operators cutting back on the fattening process, but farmers were also cutting back on the production of beef substitutes, such as chicken, pork, and eggs. Then in July all hell broke loose. In an inane attempt at keeping raw food prices down, their prices remained frozen. At the same time, most retail food ceilings were lifted. Hence, retailers and processors, but not producers, were allowed to pass on rising costs to the consumer. But here's the catch: The wholesale beef ceiling was to be kept on until September 12. The executive director of the Cost of Living's Food Committee, Kenneth Fedor, stated, "We want to manage the bulge by postponing increases." How do you think the beef industry reacted? Caught in the squeeze, some meat packers either shut down or made arrangements to do "custom slaughtering" for food chains to get around the rigid ceilings. Beef was kept off the market in anticipation of higher prices after controls were lifted.

The specter of massive meat shortages was thoroughly entrenched in the public's mind. Increased demand for storage by the public further aggravated the problem. After all, with any given supply of beef, the larger the demand, the higher is going to be the price that retailers could get. Retail beef prices continued to rise all the way up until September. The same was true for poultry and pork, for as the price of beef went up, consumers substituted relatively cheaper commodities, and hence the price of those substitutes started rising, too. Housewives everywhere were astounded at $1.00 plus a pound chickens.

But now nobody remembers the beef shortage. And in fact there is none. You can buy all the beef you want if you go to your supermarket.

The reason behind the beef crisis to start with is now quite obvious. Had the government not slapped on controls as it did, suppliers would not have withheld supplies from the market, meat packers would not have closed down, and consumers would not have attempted to inventory such large amounts of beef. The overall price index of beef, poultry, eggs and fish probably would have been lower without controls than with.

Now perhaps it is coming clear why 1973's reduction in oil supplies caused a so-called crisis. 1973 differed from 1967—or for that matter, from 1867—in that price controls had been in effect for over two years. That, of course, sounds like too simple or facile an argument. Price controls were designed presumably to help the American economy, not put it into a tail spin because of an energy shortage. Price controls, however, have been singularly unsuccessful in doing anything except creating disruptions in the economy. By now you would think that most people would be aware of this. However, they aren't; one would think that perhaps history yields no information, for the history of price controls is one of abyssmal failure whenever they were applied in any effective way.

In the year 301, for example, Roman Emperor Diocletian issued a price control edict. He boldly fixed the maximum price at which beef, grain, eggs, clothing, and other articles should be sold and prescribed the penalty of death for anyone who disposed of his wares at a higher figure. There were also wage controls then. Teachers, lawyers, physicians, bricklayers, tailors, and others could not demand a higher than prescribed salary. A Roman named Lactantius wrote in 314 that "there was . . . much bloodshed upon very slight and trifling accounts; and the people brought provisions no more to market since they could not get a reasonable price for them; and this increased the dearth so much that after many had died by it, the law itself was laid aside."

The failure of price controls that time didn't stop Emperor Julian from imposing them on grain prices in the ancient city of Antioch 60 years later. He tried to roll prices back to a level which hadn't been seen for many years, except during those in which grain was in fact in plentiful supply. Historian Edward Gibbon maintains that the results were predictable and disasterous. Merchants grabbed up corn released from the Emperial Storehouse and withheld it from the market. The small quantities that appeared in Antioch were secretly sold at high illegal prices.

In the United States, the Continental Congress imposed price controls on colonial goods with equally disasterous effects. Farmers and producers refused to sell at the lower prices. Instead, they sold their wares to the British who were willing to pay reasonable rates. The troops at Valley Forge almost starved, for this and other reasons.

Compare the situation in Germany after World War I and after World War II. In the first situation, there were no price controls; in the second situation, there were very effective ones. You'll remember that the Allies, using the Treaty of Versailles, had imposed immense reparation payments on that war-torn country after World War I. In order to finance these payments, the Weimar Republic printed marks—lots of them. By 1923 the German government was spending 12 billion marks more than it was receiving in taxes. Its expenditures were seven times as great as its revenues. The mark-U.S. dollar exchange rate went from 14 to 1 in 1919 to 4,200,000,000 to 1 in 1923! However, there were no price controls so that prices and wages adjusted rapidly to the influx of marks. In the end, there were hourly changes in prices. A strange thing occurred, though. Output in post-World War I Germany did not fall until the last six months of that country's hyperinflation. At that time, people got tired of pushing a wheelbarrow full of marks to the store just to buy a knockwurst. They finally resorted to barter.

In World War II, Nazi Germany controlled prices. So-called economic crimes, such as selling products above the maximum legal price, were immediately dealt with in a very harsh manner. When the Allies occupied Germany after the war, they didn't dismantle the rationing scheme, though they did soften the punishment somewhat. It was felt that pandemonium would have broken out in an already chaotic situation. For three years, strict price controls remained in effect. But something very strange was happening. The number of marks in circulation increased a phenomenal 400 percent during that period, while output fell by 50 percent. The mark became useless for obtaining goods and services because of widespread shortages at the controlled prices. Barter developed and commodity currencies were used. Price controls in occupied Germany were extremely successful. They were so successful that the official price index hardly budged at all. But what they did essentially was to destroy the monetary standard in that country. People in post-World War II Germany could not get any goods for their deutschmarks.

America used price controls during World War II also, as it already had to some extent during World War I. However, they were much more extensive during the Second World War and people now point out how successful they were. That may or may not be true. What certainly is true is that it was a hard job being a price-controller. In a *Playboy* interview some years ago, Professor John Kenneth Galbraith told about his days with the Office of Price Administration during World War II. At one point in the interview, Dr. Galbraith said he had decided during one trying moment in those war-torn years that it might be easier for a price of $5 to be set on everything. Such a radical idea is proof enough that the job of keeping a lid on prices during World War II must not have been easy.

What's important to remember about World War II price controls is that 1) they occurred during a period of wartime patriotism, and 2) they were administered by about 400,000 paid and volunteer price watchers scattered around the country. You also have to remember that black and gray markets were rampant during World War II. It is not clear what the true price index actually was during that period, for the official one only took account of published prices, not transactions prices. The same is true for the official price index today in the United States. What does it mean to say that prices rose only 5 percent a year when, during the last few years, there were numerous products you couldn't get at any price because producers had stopped producing them? Do you want to put a price of infinity on those products and put that into your price index? It then becomes very large indeed, right?

What never seems to be understood about price controls is that they're only effective so long as there's no reason for prices to rise anyway. As soon as there is a reason for prices to rise, they either become ineffective because people cheat, or if they are in fact strictly enforced, they become destructive, as we have all found out. Why do they become destructive? Simply because at a price set less than one which doesn't create a shortage, consumers who can get a product at that price don't have an incentive to conserve the product in question, and producers don't have enough incentive to increase production. Everybody agrees that if the price of gasoline went to $2 a gallon, people would use less. Everybody also agrees that if the price of gasoline went to $2 a gallon, producers would have an added profit incentive to increase refining capacity, to tap new wells, to increase capacity utilization of existing equipment, etc. For some reason, however, that logic is not applied to the energy question. Let's go back in time a little bit to see how effective controls on petroleum products caused distortions as far back as 1972.

First look at the problem in the context of the then-current situation. There had been, as mentioned in Chapter 2, restriction of oil imports for some time. Additionally, increased concern over the environmental implications of constructing new refineries slowed down their rate of growth. Further, there had been long-standing regulation of the price of natural gas, keeping its price below what would have prevailed otherwise. When Phase II came in, the price ceilings on fuel oil and gasoline that were established in Phase I remained in force. Herein lies the problem.

In the face of increasingly tight supplies of petroleum products generated by growing demand, the prices of refined products were not allowed to rise enough to curtail the growth in that demand, nor to stimulate additional production. Moreover, the price ceilings were set in such a way that the price of gasoline rose relative to the price of heating oil. What do you think happened? Oil companies biased their refinery production toward the more profitable product, gasoline. Shortages appeared in heating oil in the fall of 1972. And the public was warned that there might be a fuel oil crisis. To understand this better, let's go back to the August 1971 freeze.

It came at a time of seasonal weakness in the price of fuel oil and seasonal strength in the price of gasoline because less fuel oil is demanded during the summer and more gasoline. In general, the price of fuel oil rises with its usual seasonal patterns in the winter, but the winter of '71-'72 was different than all the others because the price of fuel oil was fixed. It wasn't until March 1972 that the price index of light distillates was allowed to rise from 105.4 to 106.3. But we didn't have a fuel oil crisis then because fuel oil stocks happened to be at normal levels before the price freeze. All that happened was that fuel oil inventories were drawn down below optimal levels. Now let's go to gasoline.

The gasoline price index was 102 in August of 1971 and then fell seasonally to 99.7 by February of 1972. This is a normal seasonal pattern as demand for gasoline falls in the winter and rises in the summer. The price index started to rise again into the summer so that the price of fuel oil relative to gasoline started to fall even though fuel oil prices were allowed to rise in March of '72. At the same time, the price of natural gas was allowed to rise (but not enough to prevent physical shortages at the controlled price). Industrial users started switching to fuel oil in response to the higher natural gas price and to the threatened curtailments by natural gas companies. Hence, fuel oil stocks were further depleted during this period.

Now at a time when refineries should have started refining more fuel oil, they started refining gasoline. Why? Because they were responding to the rise in the price of gasoline relative to fuel oil that was caused by government controls. Stocks of fuel oil rose much less rapidly than normal over the first 10 months of 1972. We were told that a fuel shortage would appear, and in fact it did in late fall and early winter. Denver schools had to be closed for a period because of a shortage of heating oil. Some of the corn crop was lost because oil was not available to operate corn dryers. It was fortunate that at that time the winter was mild in most parts of the country.

Then Phase III came into play. Fuel oil prices were allowed to rise in December of '72. What do you think happened? Refineries started increasing their production of fuel oil. Then people started talking about gasoline shortages in the summer.

What does this example show us? Merely that price controls can be very effective. They can be effective at getting businesses to respond to distorted price incentives. And when they are very effective, they are destructive.

For some reason, very few people are willing to lay any

blame for energy problems starting in the fall of 1973 on the existence of price controls. In fact, such people as Barry Commoner place the blame on a conspiracy among oil companies. The question is, why didn't they conspire in 1967, or why haven't they conspired at any other time period to create a crisis?

Let's assume for the moment anyway that price controls have nothing to do with our energy problems. Given, then, an absolute shortfall (isn't it great how new words spring up to meet crisis situations?) in the amount of petroleum products available, what are a country's alternatives? They are many, and only a few were ever looked at in terms of their overall effects. Now perhaps is the time to give the pros and cons on the different schemes to alleviate physical shortfalls of petroleum products, and that's the subject of the next chapter.

CHAPTER 9

Coping with Shortages

To understand current thinking we have to understand a few assumptions that policy makers consistently utilize. One is that the supply of petroleum products in the short run is for all practical purposes absolutely fixed. The other assumption is that for all practical purposes there is a constant physical minimum need for petroleum products such as gasoline and fuel oil. Given these assumptions, which are implicit in much governmental analysis of the problem, what can we do with a shortfall? Well, let's see.

One possible solution is to ration. We can either ration fuel oil or we can ration gasoline, or both. How do we do it? There are many ways it can be done. The one that was used during the Second World War was to assign everybody a ration letter. If you got an X, that meant you could get all the gas you wanted because you were a doctor or somebody like that. If you got an A, you could only get a few gallons, and if you got a B, a few more, and so on. The key to happiness was obviously getting a sticker that allowed you as much gas as you wanted to use at the controlled price and perhaps get some extra to sell to a friend at a fat profit. Now how did that work? Well, since ration coupons had to be used, it worked in a very funny manner. People didn't take very long to figure out how to cheat on the system. There were counterfeit ration coupons from the very beginning. Pretty soon the coupons started to have serial numbers, but that still didn't stop the counterfeiting. Another funny thing happened. A black market arose for ration coupons. What's a black market? The same thing as a white market except the transaction is illegal by current laws. A black market works the same way that any other market works. When people want something that is in short supply, they end up bidding a higher price for it. That price can be either in the form of an explicit monetary payment, or it can be in the form of services or goods given for free to whomever happens to have the desired resources. Black markets develop when white markets are not allowed, as people attempt to maximize their own welfare. One thing that is certain about human beings—it's difficult to get them to sacrifice their own welfare for some sort of social or public good. They might do it for a while, but it's not obvious how long (particularly if your well-connected next door neighbor does not have to do it).

What's important to note is that the implicit price of a product in scarce supply that is rationed ends up being at least as high as the price that would prevail without rationing. If this is the case, what is the benefit of rationing? Well, most people think it's important to ration during periods of scarce supply in order to prevent poor people from getting screwed. Unfortunately, no system of rationing yet presented guarantees this desired aim.

If ration coupons for gasoline, for example, are given out to people on the basis of how many cars they have, the poor, particularly the very poor who own no cars, are certainly not going to make out. If ration coupons are given to people on the basis of the number of miles driven, poor people are again certainly not going to be any better off, for the most part. The only way you can assure that poor people will in fact be better off through a rationing scheme is to give them coupons in an inverse relation to their income and allow them to sell those coupons on the open market. Then, of course, we will be redistributing income from the rich to the poor, and that perhaps is not a bad idea. But is this the way we really want to do it? It certainly seems inefficient. It would certainly seem more appropriate to give cash payments to poor people instead of involving them in a bureaucratic maze of gasoline coupons.

Actually, a rationing system puts all of the onus of reducing the shortage on the consumer. It does nothing to induce suppliers to supply any more. Now, of course, if we stick with the first assumption in this chapter, there's no way at all to increase supply in the short run. If that's indeed the case, then of course rationing at a relatively low price for gas or fuel oil will not reduce the rate of growth of supply. But there are very few things that are truly and absolutely in fixed supply. At a high enough price, you would get more resources being spent on refineries, more wells being used at more rapid rates, and so on. There was already talk of being able to increase crude oil refining capacity by 3 percent within the year following the start of the oil mess in the Middle East. If in fact there is some price responsiveness of supply of oil products even in the short run, rationing leads to *higher* implicit prices for the product than would occur otherwise, because there's no increase in supply since profit-seeking businessmen have no additional incentive at the price-controlled price to produce more.

Rationing does not appear to be the panacea that everybody thinks it is. It discourages increases in the supply and leads to black markets if white markets are not allowed to exist. The poor end up getting screwed under most rationing schemes proferred unless they are given more ration coupons proportionally to other income groups. It's hard to imagine that ever happening. We've rarely seen it happen in the past. The poor are the least organized group of any income group in society. They haven't been successful in getting much income redistributed to them in the past, and I see no reason to believe that they will be more successful today. Moreover, if you look at the numbers involved, it's not clear why the "screwing the poor" argument ever came up in the first place.

Gasoline, for example, amounts to only 2.7 percent of the typical family budget. When food prices rose by over 20 percent quite recently, nobody ever talked about rationing food, even though food amounts to about 22 percent of the typical family budget. When there was a meat crisis, nobody talked about meat rationing, but when there is an oil crisis, everybody talks about oil rationing. I don't particularly see how we can be so inconsistent in our reasoning. Is meat less important to the poor than gasoline?

Another way to cope with a physical shortfall problem as observed by the government is to either have high taxes on gasoline or have high taxes coupled with a minimum amount of ration coupons. In either case, you put all of the onus of adjustment on the consumer and give no additional incentive to the producer to find better ways of producing what the public really wants. Moreover, if you put a high tax on gasoline, you end up giving the federal government tremendous increases in revenues. If this is what you want, fine. But if you have certain objections to the way the government is spending your money already, then perhaps you'll think twice about agreeing with high taxes on gasoline products.

You must also look at the problem of the bureaucracy that's involved in any rationing system. Somebody has to make the decisions about who gets needed supplies of what. That means you have a huge army of bureaucrats trying to figure out what is essential and what isn't, be it for gasoline, fuel oil, or what have you. Whenever and wherever allocations of oil and gas become a reality, there is mayhem. And that's exactly what you would expect.

For example, in the Northwest, the government pulled out a Department of Transportation official and made him acting director of the Office of Oil and Gas Allocation. He was working with people who a few days earlier were from the Bureau of Indian Affairs, the Department of Housing and Urban Development, the Bureau of Outdoor Recreation, and other agencies. When queried about what he was going to do, the director stated, "The decision about who gets supplies will be made on who is going to get hurt the least, what effects the most people." Easier said than done. Nobody can figure out who deserves what and what's going to cause the least amount of disruption in the economy. Since the logistics of fuel oil allocation required taking employees from various other federal agencies, it was inevitable that there would be no consistent scheme utilized in any allocation program. One observer has pointed out, however, that if the social cost of government bureaucracy is a function of the number of bureaucrats, the shifting of bureaucrats from various agencies into oil and gas allocation will not cause any higher destruction to the nation. It's just a redistribution of that social waste.

More seriously, though, are the infinite number of mistakes that are possible when the rationers and allocators screw up. What happens if the allocator makes the wrong judgment and allows an entire beet crop to rot because there's no gas to dry it, or allows a corn crop to rot because there's no oil to dry the corn? The cost of these mistakes can be incredible in terms of lost output and lost jobs. In fact, the impact of the short-run reduction in crude oil shipments to the U.S. was greatly distorted, at least in the beginning, due to the existence of allocation schemes; shortages were not allowed to work themselves out as they normally would without government interference.* Everybody talked about a reverse Keynesian multiplier obtaining because of the reduction of a key input.

But ask yourself this: Is there really one key input that is so important that the whole country hinges on it? According to the stock market, that is in fact the way we view oil. The reduction of oil shipments to the United States meant a 10 to 15 percent shortfall. Total crude oil shipments in the U.S. for 1974 based at $7 per barrel of oil would have amounted to $40 billion. A reduction in that of $5 or $6 billion would mean that we had lost about 3 to 4 tenths of one percent of GNP. The stock market, however, in a five or six week period said that all manufacturing industries were worth 10 to 15 percent less because of this 4/10ths of one percent reduction. That's very hard to imagine. And, in fact, it was an overreaction, but one that was certainly consistent with the kind of disruptions that were occurring because of improper allocations and shortages. That is not to say, however, that there's a proper way to ration a scarce resource. There isn't. But there are disruptive ways, and there are ways that are less disruptive. The nondisruptive ways were used in 1967 when we had a reduction in our oil supply at home because of shipments abroad. The destructive way was used during the latest oil crisis.

It's a mistake in any event for people to think that

---

*Oil exploration even slowed down a bit because of shortages of oil (at controlled prices) to run the equipment.

something is so crucial that everything else depends on it. We made that mistake during World War II. Everybody said that if we bomb the ball bearing plants in Germany, the German war machine will come to a halt. So that's what we did and our strategic bombing maps showed that we almost eliminated the entire ball bearing production capacity of Germany. But the German war machine did not fall because of that. Why? Simply because people are ingenious in finding ways to get around problems. Nothing is absolutely crucial in a production process. And, in any event, we weren't talking about the elimination of all oil products completely. We were not talking in 1973 about the possibility of our crude oil supplies drying up 100 percent. We were only talking about at most a 20 percent reduction, and more likely a 10 percent one.

Of course, rationing, with or without additional taxes, is not the only way to handle an energy crisis. But all of the other ways suffer from many of the same problems. Take, for example, the desire to have people drive at 50 miles an hour instead of at 70. Engineers estimate that gas consumption drops by maybe 20 percent, although the estimates vary. This may be well and good if that's all you're looking at, and that may be true for private cars. One thing that's totally ignored is the increased time involved in driving, but of course if you put a zero value on everybody's time, then there's been no additional resource expended.

On the other hand, everybody agrees that 50 miles an hour is ridiculous for trucks. In fact, a speed limit that low may involve even more gas consumption, not only because their engines are tuned to run more efficiently at higher speeds, but because at 50 miles an hour they take longer to get where they're going. The same quantity of goods cannot be transported by trucks during the same time period at 50 as at 70. Hence, it requires more trucks to run to move the same quantity of goods in the same amount of time. But more trucks mean more gasoline and so, in fact, the lowered speed limit could increase truck gasoline consumption rather than decreasing it.

What about trying to get people to voluntarily use their cars less, turn their heat down, and do other things to conserve energy sources? Voluntarism works for a while, perhaps, because people think that if they can get everybody else to comply with the conservation program, they will be better off. And in fact that's true. If you get everybody else to reduce his demand for a product, you will in fact be able to get that product at a lower price and/or you may not be faced with shortages in a controlled situation. But how long can voluntarism last? Not very long, if you want to judge the present and the future by the past. Voluntarism also involves something I talked about in Chapter 5. It allows the new puritanism to rear its beautiful, make-up-free head. Even such staunchly conservative businessmen's magazines as *Business Week* started running editorials telling us that the new low-energy life style would be good for America. We have according to a *Business Week* editorial of December 1, 1973, to, "accept some fundamental changes in [our] life style." Presumably, the "U.S. economy needs a firm policy to help it adjust to the hard fact that the days of cheap energy have ended."

After all, we don't need those large gas-sucking cars; we don't need supposedly over-heated houses (even though love making at 62 degrees may not be quite as pleasureful as at 72); we don't need those trips on Sunday afternoons that were so frivolous and wasted gas; we don't need to burn our lights when we're not home just to prevent robberies; we don't need to live the way we've been living, purely and simply. No one can be denied such a value judgment. But it's one thing to make that value judgment and quite another to be in a position to impose it. But that's exactly what the energy problem created: an environment in which the public—that is, you and everyone else—would agree to let a government bureaucracy decide what you need and what you don't need. In the past, the government (for most things) didn't tell you what you needed and what you didn't need. You decided yourself. At the going price for energy, you decided how much you wanted to buy. And that never seemed to create a problem until recently. Why? Because it wasn't until recently that the government attempted to control the prices that energy, particularly oil products, were sold at.

I predicted from the beginning that when controls were ended or eased as they were almost immediately when the "crisis" occurred, there would be no more crisis. After all, nobody remembers the beef shortage any more, and it went away as soon as controls were ended there. Why is energy any different? Now some people say it's different because we're running out, but we handled that problem in Chapter 6 already. We're running out of everything, but we always have been. Why does it have to be 1973 or '74 or '75 when all of a sudden we realize that we are almost to the bottom of the well? In fact, if you look at the statistics given us by the oil industry, for example, we have more proven reserves now than we had 35 years ago. But that really is irrelevant. The way to get people to conserve on a resource that is becoming more scarce is not to ration it to them—because that becomes arbitrary, messy, and allows the government to control our life styles—but rather to force people to 'fess up to the true costs of their consumption. And the way we generally do that is to make them pay more.

Now you may complain that that hurts the poor and, indeed, it might, although gasoline accounts for a very small percentage of the poor's budget. Nonetheless, we can devise programs to help the poor in a way that will not distort the situation for everybody else. One of these programs, of course, would be cash payments. The poor, after all, are basically poor because they don't have any income, or not much to speak of. In the short run, the way to solve that problem is to give them what they need— money. In the long run, the way to solve the problem is to give them better education and better opportunities for making higher incomes. And also, by the way, we could eliminate many of the restrictions that prevent them from working, such as discriminatory union hiring practices.

Now everybody agrees that the energy bought by consumers and industry has been selling at too low a price because pollution has been involved and nobody's been paying for it. One of the proposed solutions to the energy problem today has been to ease up pollution requirements for the burning of oil, for example, and coal—that is, reduce the sulfur oxide restrictions. This certainly will increase the supply of energy sources. The same would be true if we were allowed to disconnect all of the pollution control devices on automobiles and put off instituting pollution abatement requirements that are to go into effect in the future. Now this may be advisable if it's finally figured out that the cost of additional pollution equipment on cars is not worth the benefits. But unless that is shown to be the case, there is no reason to go back to pre-pollution legislation situations.

The pollution issue is separate from the energy crisis. It must be decided on its own merits. If we have determined that we are willing to pay the price of a cleaner environment, so be it. That doesn't mean, however, that this wouldn't be a good time to reexamine some of the legislation, such as the Clean Water Act, the Clean Air Act, and so on. A lot of people have been grumbling about the arbitrariness of the standards being set for industry and automobiles, pointing out that the costs in fact are not matched by the benefits. In any event, don't give in on pollution controls just because of a temporary tight supply situation from an energy source.

Basically, then, it's pretty hard to come up with an effective, equitable, and nondestructive solution to what is considered to be a physical shortfall in something like oil. But it's a mistake in the first place to talk about energy needs as if those needs were some physical constant. If we had predicted our energy needs 30 years ago, we certainly would have no problem today, but nobody anticipated the tremendous rate of growth in the consumption of energy in the United States. How can one justify the concept of a physical need for a scarce resource other than what is biologically necessary for survival when those needs seem to change all the time and in a manner that most people don't anticipate? The physical need for energy predicted for the next ten years is based on current consumption patterns, current relative prices for energy, and current supply techniques with currently discovered resources.

Any one of those things can change, and the key to understanding how the quantity of energy demanded may change is to realize that it can be at any level you want it to be at. Raise the price of electricity to 20 times what it is today, and you can be certain that the quantity demanded will fall. Lower the price to 1/20th of what it is today and the quantity demanded will rise. Somehow this seems to be ignored, although those who are a little more sophisticated in their analysis maintain that this is well and good in the long run, but not in the short run. In the short run, they say, the price responsiveness of demand for, say, electricity is effectively zero; hence, to eliminate a shortage, the price rise would have to be tremendous. This is an empirical question, and one that numerous researchers have been studying for years. Note also that if people demand exactly the same quantity of, say, electricity, even when its price rises, that must mean the quantity demanded is an absolute physical necessity. Hence, curbing its use by even a small amount through rationing, etc., presumably will mean total disaster. Estimates, however, of the short-run price responsiveness of electricity have ranged as high as 1.1. That is, a one percent increase in the price of electricity will yield a 1.1 percent decrease in the quantity demanded. That certainly is a different situation than a zero price responsiveness where, for example, a 50 percent increase in the price would not alter the quantity demanded one bit. Others make the same assumptions about the demand for gasoline and the demand for fuel oil. Empirically, it does not appear that this is really the case. When the price of gas goes up, people find millions and millions of ways to conserve it—by driving less, by shifting into higher gears earlier, by not flooring the accelerator, by going in car pools, by tuning the engine better, by driving slower on the highway, by taking buses, by taking trains, and so on.

Never underestimate the ingenuity of an American (or a Frenchman or an Englishman or a Swede, for that matter) in figuring out a way to conserve on something that becomes more expensive. The same is true for fuel oil. Everybody says that if the price goes up, in the short run people will still demand the same amount. But that can't be true because people can find ways to reduce their consumption. If the price goes up, they will of their own accord lower their thermostats, put on automatic stop-start controls to cut off the heater during the night, put in storm windows, keep their drapes pulled, install insulation in the attic, and so on. The number of ways that one can conserve is tremendous. They don't have to be dictated by some government official who prescribes savings only on some of these, and then applies them blindly to everyone.

They never have been dictated in the past, and it's hard to find a reason why they should be today or tomorrow.

Now this does not mean that the consumer wouldn't be better off if he were provided with more information about how he could voluntarily reduce his energy consumption. For example, air conditioners that are rated in terms of electricity usage would indicate which was the least costly to run. Builders could specify the different trade-offs between more insulation and less heating costs, and so on. But again, information is a scarce resource, just like oil. You wouldn't particularly want to have the government require tremendous amounts of such information, because after a certain point the additional value received from that information is not worth the cost. Anyhow, when the price of fuel oils doubles, you can be sure that builders will be quick to advertise their double windows and well insulated homes; manufacturers of air conditioners efficient in electricity use will be quick to draw attention to these features of their product when the price of electricity skyrockets.

CHAPTER 10

Self-Sufficiency by 1980

That's the new expression for the 1970s. Let's make sure we don't rely on any of those nasty foreigners to supply us with something so crucial as oil. Let's be self-sufficient by 1980. Sounds like a good idea, doesn't it? But when you think about it, this notion goes against everything that economists have ever realized about the nature of economics. Self-sufficiency as an argument in and of itself is the same thing as isolationism. Self-sufficiency is the same thing as saying let's not specialize; let's not take advantage of the gains from trade; let's go it on our own. A common expression that categorizes this type of thinking is "cutting off one's head to spite one's nose." We'll show those crummy Mideast oil men. We won't need any of their oil by 1980. We'll get it ourselves. If we go ahead with this policy, and it looks like we will, the American people will be worse off, not better off.

First consider the reason why you do any business with anybody else. Obviously, you enter into voluntary exchanges because you think you will be better off. So, too, does the other party. Voluntary exchange must make both parties better off (at least subjectively) or no exchange would take place. The reason people, since the beginning of history, have wanted to exchange things with other people is to make themselves better off. And the reason they have wanted to make themselves better off is because they haven't had all of the goods and services they would have liked to have had in their lives. And why is that? Simply because we have now, always have had, and always will have a limited amount of resources. We live in a world of scarcity.

If we didn't live in a world of scarcity, you wouldn't have to think about the economic aspects of anything because there wouldn't be any. Scarcity presents us with a problem: How do we allocate the available resources to all the competing demanders of those resources? For indeed there are many people in competition for scarce goods and services. And even if they decided not to really compete, they would still face the problem of how the available resources were to be allocated among members of society. So you see, it really doesn't matter what the situation is. Everybody can love everybody else and want to help everybody else, but the decision still has to be made: Who gets what and how much?

Most of you do not have everything you want, and so you have to decide what to do with your productive talents. In general, if you want to make yourselves as well off as possible, you will apply your talents to productive endeavors which yield the highest rewards. Now it is true that part of this reward can be psychic. For the moment, forget about psychic rewards that people get from doing different jobs. Look only at money rewards.

Now it's pretty easy for you to figure out what you do comparatively better than other people. All you have to do is look at your alternatives. You decide what you can do best by finding out which productive endeavor gives you the highest rate of return for the time spent working—i.e., the highest command over those goods and services which you would like to consume. Then you specialize in this endeavor. This is the famous economic principle of specialization. It applies not only to individuals, but to states and to nations as well. The history of the development of any country in the world, including the United States, is in fact a history of specialization.

Specialization through the division of labor rests on a very important fact—different people, different communities, and different nations are indeed different, at least when it comes to the ability of each to produce goods and services. Take the simplest example, a two person society. If each person were exactly the same in every respect, and hence, each person could do every job just as well as the other one, there would obviously be less reason for specialization. The same is true for nations. If every nation had exactly the same resources and exactly the same talents, then the cost of producing any good or service would be pretty much the same everywhere. There would be little need or incentive to specialize, particularly if every nation had the same set of tastes. However, costs do differ. It is relatively less costly, for instance, for Japan to specialize in the production of, say, electronic equipment than it is for the United States under current circumstances. We say that Japan's current comparative advantage lies in the production of electronic equipment. The principle of specialization rests on the existence—the actual fact—of comparative advantage. We know that it exists because we know that different people and different countries experience different relative costs of producing different goods and services.

Now you will all agree that trade within the United States is a good thing. In fact, the founders of the Constitution set it up so as to prohibit all interferences with trade within the United States. If you can accept that fact, why is it so difficult to accept the fact that trade among nations is also beneficial? Nonetheless, ever since Abraham Lincoln sprouted his now-famous words, "If I buy a Nikon, I have a camera and Japan has my money, but if I buy a Kodak, I have the camera and America has the money," men have decided that trade among nations is not always beneficial. Hence, trade barriers have been set up continuously and in just about every country of the world. They are designed to "protect" domestic industry. While it is true that they protect particular industries, they hurt general economic welfare. After all, the reason we trade is because we can purchase goods and services we want from other countries at a lower price than it costs to produce them here. In exchange, we give other countries those goods and services which we can produce relatively more cheaply than they can. Exports from the United States are the means of payment for the relatively inexpensive imports which we bring into the country. The greater the volume of trade possible, the greater the degree of specialization and the higher the economic value received from a given amount of resources. That doesn't seem to be the way Nixon, his advisers, and energy people are thinking, at least not any more. For the notion of being self-sufficient in energy by 1980 goes against all of the above arguments in favor of unconstrained trade among nations.

Look at it this way. If oil in the Middle East were costing $2.50 per barrel to us, would it not be to our advantage to purchase that oil instead of, for example, to develop an Alaska oil supply where it costs us $4 or $5 a barrel? Now obviously once the OPEC countries started raising the price and restricting the supply, that was no longer possible. But as we mentioned many times throughout this book, that agreement is not going to last forever. The incentive for chiselling is too great and it will break down. We will eventually be able to buy that oil again at prices well below the cost of pumping it out of Alaska, or the North Sea for that matter.

But, you say, what about the possibility of a future cut-off of oil, or what if we never get any oil again from the Middle East? What if they keep an embargo on indefinitely? That still is not an argument for self-sufficiency in energy by 1980. The market, of course, has ways of handling this. If I want safe fuel supplies for my operations, I will have a long-term contract with a reliable seller. Since the Mideast sellers are not reliable, they will have to bear the penalty of a lower price. A local producer could get the contract and would expand his productive capacity accordingly.

There are numerous other sources of energy supplies that are cheaper than our own domestic development of those same supplies, however. We benefit by purchasing those less expensive resources and using our own scarce resources to produce what we can produce comparatively cheaper than anyone else. Now it is true that if we have self-sufficiency in energy, we rely on no one else, and hence we cannot be hurt by temporary curtailment of energy shipments to the United States. But what a price we'll have to pay for this certainty! We have to ask ourselves if we really want to pay it.

The way we can find out if we're willing to pay the price is by looking at the additional use of resources necessary to make ourselves self-sufficient in energy by 1980. Add up all of these costs from now until eternity, then do an alternate projection. Project out the costs of *not* being self-sufficient in energy and instead, importing supplies for our energy needs. Put in the probability of any one year seeing an oil embargo, and the resultant cost to us of that embargo. Don't make the mistake, however, of seeing what happened in 1973 and '74, and then deciding that the costs of a reduction in oil shipments are too high.

Look back to 1967 and see what happened when we lost part of our oil supply (since we sold it to Europe). Then the result was not a crisis, but rather a rise in the price of petroleum products. That's the true cost of a reduction in oil shipments, not the chaos that has occurred (and certainly has been overexaggerated) due to the inability of the government to make the millions of decisions that are required every day. And of course, the reason the government was put in a position to make those decisions is because we had been living under a reign of price controls, thereby causing distortions everywhere and exacerbating the tightness of fuel supplies.

Now, compare the costs of the two systems, the one where we go to total self-sufficiency by 1980, and the other where we purchase as many energy supplies from abroad as is profitable. That is, one alternative system is no trade in energy supplies, and the other is unrestrained trade in energy supplies. I don't think there's any doubt about which system would give Americans a higher standard of living.

There are two arguments against my point of view here, and they are worth considering again, although we've touched on them briefly before. One is the national defense argument; the other is the effect of large oil imports on international monetary problems.

If indeed it is true that we need a certain quantity of oil to feed our military machine in time of war, that still does not necessarily mean we have to be energy self-sufficient by 1980. The alternatives to energy self-sufficiency are many. For example, we can store oil underground or above ground at perhaps 70¢ per barrel per year. That's not an outrageous cost when you realize that we're not talking about storing our entire supply of oil, but only that fraction which comes from abroad. And even then we're not talking about the total fraction; we're talking about a particular quantity that would be required to keep the military happy.*

Let's put an oil embargo in perspective. In 1973 an oil embargo merely meant that oil supplies would be the same as they were in 1970. In 1970 nobody was talking about an oil crisis, so in 1973 all it would have meant is that consumption levels would have to be reduced to what they were three years earlier. One can only go so far with the national defense argument in support of total reliance on domestic sources of energy. The alternatives are relatively costless and available to provide all of the energy needs in time of war in case we are cut off from foreign supplies. The cost of doing that in the name of national defense is certainly going to be much lower than cutting ourselves off from the rest of the world's relatively cheap sources of energy.

On to the other point. Projections from the State Department and energy experts indicate that by 1980, if present trends continue, Arab oil countries will be getting huge multi-billion dollar payments from us every week. And, so the story goes, since they don't need the money, they can use it as a political tool. They can use it to disrupt international money markets, to cause stock markets to plummet in different parts of the world, and in all sorts of other devious tricks. We've already taken care of both of these arguments before, but since they're so popular, we'll look at them again. In the first place, it's an absurd argument to say that the Arab countries don't need any more money. There's some assumption that that money is going to be useless later on. But why is that so? Don't you and I save so that we can consume in the future? Isn't it possible for oil-rich Arab countries to invest whatever they don't "need" today so that they can consume in the

---

*Some say that might be an infinite quantity.

future at a higher level? The answer is obviously yes. Their oil reserves are not infinite. Some day they will run out, or some day they might even be worthless if a substitute is found, just as was the case with whale oil.

In any event, the widow's cruse is not without a bottom. The Arabs are no different than anybody else. They can take all income that they don't "need" today or tomorrow or the next day and invest it. Or if they don't mind not earning any interest, they can just keep it in cash or in a checking account somewhere. It will be available for use in the future. What will they do with it? The same thing that they do with it today: spend it on goods and services. Everybody considers Arab countries part of the underdeveloped sector of the world; what's all this nonsense about them not needing any money? Actually, it doesn't matter if they were the richest countries in the world. They will always have the opportunity of spending it later.

Aha! But they'll be able to disrupt financial markets around the world. Perhaps, but it certainly doesn't seem like it will be in their best interests to do so. In a world of floating exchange rates, which is more or less what we have now, there will be no effect on the balance of payments because of our supposedly excessive imports of oil from abroad. In a world of floating exchange rates there's no such thing as a balance of payments problem because the exchange rate adjusts to make the balance of payments always balance. We're eventually getting to that situation unless of course the international bankers are able to get us back on the insidious regime of fixed (i.e., rationed) prices for foreign currencies. Hopefully this will never happen. We suffered enough under a system of rigid exchange rates where we had crises with money just like those with oil.

In any event, in a world of floating exchange rates, there's no balance of payments problem and it would probably not pay an Arab country to attempt to disrupt the financial monetary markets. After all, the Arab countries will be looking for investment opportunities elsewhere, and those investment opportunities will be more attractive the more stable the international monetary situation. It's difficult to believe that out of sheer power-craziness, Arab leaders will cut their own throats by causing international monetary chaos, even if that were possible. And if they attempt to cause trouble, they'll have to pay a penalty in terms of a lower rate of earnings as compared with a stable investor.

But what about the possibility of disrupting stock markets around the world? Presumably, if the Arabs have so much money, they would be able to buy substantial fractions of stocks in different countries, drive the price up, and then sell out and let the bottom fall out of the market. If this were indeed the case, how long do you think it would take people to catch on? Every time Arab countries started buying big blocks of stock, financial wizards would know that they were going to pull out in the future and the price would fall. These financial wizards would do the obvious: sell short. But we know that selling short is a stabilizing factor in a stock market. For eventually those who sell short have to buy in order to pay off the stocks they sold. And when they buy, they prevent the price from falling.

In short, the arguments for limiting our reliance on foreign oil supplies are weak at best. Nonetheless, they are being used as an excuse for ever-increasing taxpayers' payments to research and development (R & D) programs for energy in the United States.

Of course, there are plenty of reasons why we would all like to see cheap energy in the U.S., whether it comes from breeder reactors, nuclear fusion, shale oil, coal gasification, or what have you. But that doesn't automatically call for a massive public energy development program. Generally, public programs are called for only when the benefits exceed the costs. That may or may not be the case, but it is certainly not true that the possibility of another oil embargo can be the *raison d'etre* of massive increases in R & D funds for the development of future energy sources.

The reason that the energy industry has asked the Congress for more R & D funds is obvious: Private companies always think they'll benefit if they can get public funds for their research. Most private companies will never turn down a subsidy. Shouldn't you be suspicious of something that is tauted as so necessary by private oil, gas and electric companies? After all, they seem to be the villains in everybody's mind. Why do we suddenly listen when they tell us that the government has to pay for their R & D research because they can't "afford" to do it? This is just another area where for some reason the bad guys become the good guys and they're on our side. I find that inconsistent. If we assume that energy companies are out to make the most money possible, why should we believe their propaganda about what the government should do with taxpayers' money? The private companies are going to get busy lobbying so that taxpayers' money is used to their benefit, not ours. That's just simple profit-maximizing behavior.

Did we ever believe in the past that energy companies were providing us with energy for our own good, or for the good of society at large? Should we ever believe the ads that energy companies put out telling us that they're not in the business of producing energy, but of producing clean rivers and clear skies? It's always best to assume that private companies are out for private gain, not public welfare. In any event, the argument for massive public funds for energy R & D is weak, just as weak as the argument for being totally self-sufficient. When the rate of return is high enough, private energy companies will start expanding their own R & D efforts, just like they have done in the past. And when the projects are huge, such as that for nuclear fusion, that just means that a number of them will have to chip in to a common kitty. If we spend more money than is socially optimal today for energy R & D, we are worse off in the future, not better off, even though we might have cheaper energy supplies. We are worse off because we've wasted resources getting to that cheap energy situation—we pay by giving up excessively in lost consumption or in reduced alternative investments today. Don't let the motto of the seventies be "We're going to have cheap energy no matter what it costs us."

Some people like to use the argument that private companies are short-sighted, that they are unwilling to take account of public needs in the future. This is typically the argument used, for example, to put government bureaucrats in charge of allocation programs so as to conserve scarce resources. After all, the government bureaucrat will look out for the general public, whereas the private entrepreneur will look out only for himself. That's a strange piece of reasoning, indeed. Look at the incentives facing the two different decision-makers. In the first instance, you have a private entrepreneur who has to make decisions about future demands and supplies for whatever he owns. For example, if he owns natural gas (in an unrestricted situation) he has to figure out what the costs of exploration will be in the future, what the demand will be in the future (and this is a function of what substitutes are available and their prices), what the costs of production will be in the future, and so on. He has to use all this information in deciding what quantity of natural gas to sell at the going price. Now let's say that he screws up. He underestimates the demand for natural gas in the future. Now he will have made a big mistake because he will have sold too much gas today and he won't have enough in the future. And how will he know he made that mistake? Easily. His profits will be lower than they would have been otherwise. His net worth will be lower. The same thing holds if he makes a mistake on the other side of the coin. If he overestimated the demand for natural gas in the future, he will have sold too little today, and again his profits will be lower than they would have been otherwise, and his net worth will therefore also be lower. In other words, he has a direct incentive to make correct decisions, to spend an optimal amount of resources to estimate future demands and supplies for his product.

On the other hand, look at the incentives facing a government bureaucrat. Let's say he wants to take account of the same supply and demand as the private entrepreneur. Now what incentives does he have to make a correct decision and to spend the optimal amount of time and money getting the right information? Well, if his estimates of the future demand for natural gas are underestimates, then he allows too much to be sold today, just as did the private entrepreneur. What's the worst that can happen when this is found out? He can lose his job perhaps (but certainly not if he is a civil servant), he can be shamed in public, and so on. It's not clear, though, how much his net worth position will fall. He can probably go to another office, and this happens all the time. On the other hand, what about the possibility of his overestimating the demand for natural gas? Now here he's in a better position because even though he will have allowed too little to be sold today, he won't look so bad in the future, because he can always say that the "surplus" is appropriate for the sake of conservation. Again, he doesn't lose out very much if he makes an incorrect decision. In fact, he might even be a hero. Hence the probability is much higher, of course, that he will overestimate the future demand for the product he's in charge of than that he will underestimate because a surplus doesn't look as bad as a shortage since it can always be explained away as a conservation measure.

It is beyond me why people think that government bureaucrats whose net worth position does not depend so directly on the correctness of their decisions about the use of resources do any better than private decision-makers. Nonetheless, they are always asked to make the decision, particularly with respect to natural resources. They are being asked to make the decisions now with respect to the optimal level of R & D for energy. Why should we expect them to do a better job than anybody else? In fact, we should expect them to overestimate the demand for energy in the future so as to make sure that there is no energy "shortage." This way, even though public monies will have been wasted, the bureaucrats in charge of the programs will come out smelling like roses; they will be hailed as the conquering heroes, conquering nature and providing abundance of energy once again. In the aggregate, you and I will lose, not gain, from such behavior.

Carrying the same analysis of individual maximization to its limits, we can come up with a startling picture of how Richard Nixon might have created the crisis atmosphere that the public was subjected to in '73 and '74. Remember, though, it's all a theory that you're about to read, and anybody in government will consistently deny that there's a ghost of a chance that it be true. If you want, treat it as another fairy tale. (Then relabel it Chapter 00.)

CHAPTER 11

Nixon's Greatest Coup (Maybe)

Perhaps you remember the 1968 campaign, or the 1972 campaign. Certainly in 1968, conservatives everywhere jumped on the Nixon bandwagon. He was going to be their savior. He was going to return the nation to an unrestricted economic society where the market forces of supply and demand would be used throughout to determine the best allocation of our scarce resources. Restrictions in the marketplace would disappear. Government programs that bred inefficiency would be eliminated. And decentralization of the entire governing apparatus would occur. By 1972, it was obvious that nothing of the kind had happened. We still had wage and price controls, and very few government programs had been eliminated, although the federal government's budget had not risen as rapidly as in the past. Free market conservatives had a hard time justifying another vote for Richard Nixon, but the alternative, George McGovern, seemed even worse. Even conservatives who were staunchly against Nixon's handling of the Vietnam fiasco were convinced to vote again for the man who sooner or later would get the nation back on the road to free enterprise. I can even remember a short but instructive conservation with the Honorable George Schultz in October of 1972. My question about "What's happened to Richard Nixon?" was answered with a firm and convincing "Mr. Nixon really does believe in free enterprise. We'll get back to it soon." By then, however, I, along with some 200 million other Americans, had realized that what Richard Nixon says and what Richard Nixon does are not often the same thing.

He was elected using conservative slogans. He preached nonintervention in the marketplace. He consistently came out against wage and price controls. He even said that he had been in the Office of Price Administration during World War II and he knew that controls couldn't work. Nonetheless, we got wage and price controls. When the Economic Stabilization Act was running out, he told Congress he wanted it renewed. He promised, however, that he would not use it again. He just wanted to have it there. But he did use it again. In the fall of 1973, he told us that he would never use rationing. Three days after that announcement, the news media picked up the story that indeed fuel oil rationing was going to occur and it was just a matter of time before gasoline was affected also. What is amazing is that people continued, and perhaps still do, to believe Nixon when he says something.

Everybody ate up Watergate. They all said, "Oh, if we had only voted in good guy George McGovern, this never would have happened." The negative comments about the veracity of Richard Nixon numbered in the millions. Nonetheless, people still seemed to ignore the fact that an exorbitant quantity of his statements were proven false by his own actions or those of his lieutenants in all matters— be they economic, political, or otherwise.

It was also interesting to witness the reversal in his popularity right in the midst of the entire Watergate scandal. How could this have happened? Well, you will see that according to one theory, Nixon may have pulled off his greatest coup ever. Anyway, during the Watergate proceedings, the energy crisis loomed large. All of a sudden, the president found himself not with reduced powers, which is exactly what he expected to have because of his lack of support since Watergate, but increased powers. The Congress gave him—nay, forced on him, according to some observers—the power to ration petroleum products. A week before he was called a crook, then he was given the power over a crucial product used by all of us.

The public flocked to his feet to listen to his pronouncements about how the president's office was going to solve the energy crisis. All of a sudden, we needed the president, even if he happened to be the same one who was involved in the Watergate scandal, and who—even though it wasn't proven at the time—was considered guilty by a large percentage of Americans.

This occurred even at a time when things were happening such as the famous 18 minute blank in a Watergate tape. Nixon's secretary maintained that she, uh, er, oh, accidently erased it. Now those of you who know what a tape recorder is, know that it is generally pretty difficult to erase 18 minutes of a tape without knowing it, particularly when you're not recording anything, but just playing stuff back. Generally, you have to push at least two buttons to get the record-erase mechanism to operate because tape recorder manufacturers know that tape recorder users don't particularly like to make the mistake of erasing already recorded tape unless they want to. Hence, fail safe mechanisms are usually put into the tape recorder to prevent such disasters. But we were supposed to believe it was all a "mistake."

A lot of people were saying a lot of nasty things about Nixon after the Watergate scandal came out. How could he be so stupid, some muttered. But they were soon to see that whatever he was, stupid he was not. What is the one thing that brings a nation to unity? What is the one thing that brings a nation to rally behind its leaders? Crisis. What happened in the fall of 1973 just when there was increasing pressure for Nixon to resign and the impeachment proceedings were starting to get hot? A crisis. It happened to be the energy crisis, but it could have been any crisis. And before that, of course, it was the Middle East crisis itself where the president took strong action with the Sixth Fleet, or whatever it was. It was only a matter of weeks after the energy "crisis" really got underway before Richard Nixon was actually joking with the press about his impeachment. And it was a matter of weeks before the American public started to think that Richard Nixon wasn't so bad at all. In fact, newscasters started saying, "Think twice now about impeaching the man who is going to save us from this crisis." The popularity polls showed an about-face in public support for the president. Whether or not this turn around will prove sufficient to keep Mr. Nixon in office of course only history will tell. But the facts were there. It started to work from the very beginning.

Now, is it possible that the president manufactured the crisis to save his own skin? No, you say, how could he manufacture the shortfall in oil supplies? Obviously, he could not manufacture that because that was a physical fact. But the same thing happened in 1967 and we didn't have a crisis. What we had was a rise in the price of petroleum products that people complained about, but somehow adjusted to. It's hard to imagine that the president did not know what he was doing when he was imposing price controls in 1971, and it's hard to imagine he did not know what he was doing when he kept those controls on even after it was obvious to him that we were going to lose a small but significant portion of our imported oil.

After all, he has economic advisers around him who must have been telling him all along the consequences of price controls in an inflationary setting when aggregate demand policies on the part of the government continue to be expansionary (albeit intermittently). After all, he had a Chairman of the Council of Economic Advisers who submitted a very satirical letter to the editor of the New York *Times* making fun of the possibility of rationing meat during the "meat shortage." After all, he had a Secretary of the Treasury who coedited a book on wage and price controls taken from a conference at the University of Chicago, a book in which the hard facts of life were presented by the various scholars present at that conference. After all, he had advisers who told him that one way to cut off demand for gasoline was to slap a 40¢ tax per gallon on it. Obviously, these advisers knew that when the price of something goes up, the quantity demanded falls, so that if a tax were slapped on gasoline, people individually would find ways to conserve it because it had become more expensive.

It is very difficult to imagine that Mr. Nixon did not know that his price controls policy would result in a "shortfall" and subsequent energy crisis starting in the fall of 1973 after the oil embargo. Hence, if he did know what he was doing, the crisis was artificially created in order to get the people to rally around their fallen leader. The importance of the presidency increased about five million fold in a very short time, for everyone believed that the only salvation was through the presidency. In fact, reporters were demanding to know why the president hadn't taken steps earlier to prevent an energy crisis. In other words, everybody believed, and probably still does, that only the federal government can help us out in our energy problems, when in fact—as I think it has become obvious to you—the federal government is at the heart of the problem. The particular institutional changes, such as the loss of 10 percent of our oil, only made the problem more acute and got people thinking in terms of it being a crisis. But this is exactly what the government, including the head of the ship, would want.

Do you realize the powers that were taken over in the name of national welfare during the energy crisis? Would you ever have believed that the federal government would be telling you how warm to heat your house, how fast to drive your car, how many lights to leave on? But everybody accepted that as a necessary way to get us out of a crisis when the crisis supposedly started in the fall of 1973.

What is obvious is that without a crisis, nobody would have had any special reason to increase their support for the presidency. In fact, people were just beginning to realize that perhaps it wasn't the man, Richard Nixon, they should be worrying about, but the amount of power that they slowly but surely had relinquished to the federal government. Eric Hoffer once said that what is great about America is not its presidents, but the fact that it can get along without a president. At first, right after Watergate, the American public bemoaned their choice of a president. McGovern presumably wouldn't have done anything so dishonest. Eventually, however, the real truth came out: power corrupts, as Lord Acton astutely pointed out many years ago, and absolute power corrupts absolutely. No matter who is president, if you give that person the opportunity to wield power, he will sooner or later take advantage of it. The way to avoid Watergate fiascos is to take away the power that whoever is in office can wield.

The energy "crisis" turned that thinking around 180 degrees. After it started, the public was hoodwinked into believing that only the Office of the President and the president himself could help us in our moment of dire need. Otherwise, the lights might go out forever and the American way of life would crumble.

A fantastic story? Maybe. A fairy tale? Perhaps. A possibility? Don't write it off. While the president was meeting with his advisers to talk rationing problems, the price controllers were quietly allowing the price of gasoline and fuel oil to rise once a month by a few cents a gallon. In fact, on December 1, 1973, fuel oil cost about 50 percent more than it had a year earlier. By January 1, 1974, it was up again. What does that mean for fuel oil? That means another 50 percent increase was possible in the first six months of 1974. Lo and behold, the public would react to that price increase in the millions of ways it knew how to react, in the millions of ways it could conserve on fuel oil. The same was true with gasoline. And as oil product prices started to rise, oil companies were getting ready to release stored crude for refining. That's right. There was crude being kept off the market during the "crisis." Why? For the same reason that beef was kept off the market during the beef "crisis." Because sellers knew that controls were temporary. They were waiting for a higher price in the future.

Lo and behold, there was to be no oil crisis (if nothing else changed) in much less than a year after it all started. Richard Nixon was planning to tell everybody he pulled us out of the crisis, he got us through the storm. He was to become the conquering hero. At least that's one notion of the way he was thinking when it all started to begin with. Perhaps history will prove this scenario totally wrong, but the possibility exists and should not be ignored. For if there's any validity to it at all, you have been taken for one long sleigh ride during an unair-conditioned July.

CHAPTER 12

A Positive Program
for the Future

It's obviously too late to change anything that's already happened. Bygones must be bygones. But it's never too late to improve the future. It's never too late to get America back on the path of rational energy resource use. It's never too late to get us back onto the road of sane management of our natural resources. It's useless for us to bemoan the fact that we've wasted so much in the past. Now is not the time to wear hair shirts and to come out in massive public support for all those who tell us we're profligate energy pigs. That argument doesn't hold water, and is irrelevant anyway. All of us are going to react in our own individual ways to make ourselves as well off as possible, and we react to whatever signals are given to us. If somebody sells us a killowatt of electricity below its social cost, we're going to use more of it than we would if the price were higher. If somebody tells us there's a physical shortfall in oil and gives us ration coupons to drive our cars, about half of us are going to trade them so that those who want the gas the most will end up using the most and in the process bidding either the explicit or implicit price up. That's the world in which we live and unless human nature changes tomorrow, we're stuck with it. Since we're stuck with it, we have to work around it. And in so doing, we can come up with a program to rationalize the energy picture. Now it may not mean an era of abundant energy forever. It may not mean that you'll never have to pay a high price for something you "need." What it will mean, though, is that we'll use our resources wisely and we'll never be confronted with the absurdity of an artificial crisis compounding the original one, like the one that was whipped up in 1973 and '74 (and perhaps even later).

First, *eliminate all special privileges to the oil industry.* Nobody's heart bleeds for oil men, and now is not the time to become hemopheliacs just because you think we need them so much. They're out to maximize their own interests, not yours and not mine. In so doing, the numerous oil companies end up competing against themselves in such a way that they can't keep prices of oil arbitrarily high—that is, higher than the costs of production plus a profit—unless there's government intervention. Cut out the nonsense of ever restricting imports to help out oil companies. In the future, foreign oil prices may fall again and you can be sure that oil companies are going to ask for an oil import program to keep prices in the U.S. propped up. There's no reason in the world to give special tax advantages, moreover, to the oil industry. Get rid of oil depletion allowances; get rid of full costing of dry holes off other income; get rid of special capital gains tax treatment; get rid of the costing provision for IDCs; get rid of prorationing of oil by absurd agencies such as the Texas Railroad Commission. Don't support the oil industry, for it is not special. It is no different than any other industry. We'll get all the oil that is socially desirable without special provisions to help oil companies out. They respond to rising prices just like any other companies, by producing more, because that's how they increase their profits.

Second, *get rid of the price regulation of natural gas.* It has been senseless for natural gas prices to be artificially low for so many years. Of course, there were no problems when the prices were first fixed because there wasn't much inflation and there weren't pollution controls that caused people to desire to burn cleaner fuels. But we've had inflation, and we've had pollution standards set for electric utilities and other industries. The demand for natural gas exceeds the supply at the current controlled price, even though that price has been allowed to go up a little bit in the past few years. The truth is obvious: Electric utilities are willing to buy dollar plus (per thousand cubic feet) liquified natural gas from Algeria and other places, while the domestically produced stuff sells for much less but is not always available. Obviously it's worth a lot more to them than the FPC-controlled price. (By the way, the arbitrarily controlled price for interstate shipments caused inefficiency because of an overuse of natural gas for intrastate purposes.) In any event, a decontrolled price of natural gas would cause many natural gas companies to increase their exploration; it would cause others to take the caps off already discovered wells. The supply would increase, thereby taking the pressure off other energy sources. Even the president was crying for the decontrolling of natural gas at the beginning of the so-called energy crisis.

Because of low (controlled) prices, gas companies found themselves in the uncomfortable position of *priority rating*; they had to decide whose gas service would be interrupted when the supply ran out. Now, isn't that ridiculous? How can you tell who "deserves" natural gas more than somebody else? It was ludicrous to read the hearings for establishing priorities within natural gas companies. You can't blame them for doing what they had to do, but the arguments were absurd. How can anybody tell whether somebody's demand for natural gas for, say, a home water heater is more important than are natural gas demands for a home stove, or an industrialist's demands for producing his products?

Third, *institute a peak load pricing system for the sale of electricity.* One of the big reasons we have brownouts and blackouts is because we have a single rate pricing system for electricity, the demand for which is not constant throughout the day or throughout the year. Why do you think it usually costs more to get into a night club on the weekend than during the week? Because on the weekend the demand is higher. To ration a fixed number of seats in a night club, owners charge more—a cover charge. This also has the desired effect of getting some people to come during the week when the night club is less crowded. The same would be true for electricity. At a high enough price during peak periods, businesses, for example, would find ways to cut down electricity use and to shift it to nonpeak periods when the price is cheaper. You might even find plants operating at night instead of during the day to save electricity. The increased wages they would have to give workers for working at night would be more than compensated for by the electricity savings.

A lot of people say this won't work because people "need" all the electricity they use. That's nonsense. Nobody's had the courage to try it. Obviously, public utility commissioners are going to have to have their arms twisted to do this, because they don't want to see prices rise. But as was mentioned before, the excess profits earned by the electric utility could be taxed away or put into a trust fund for expansion only (on which they will still earn their normal profits). Peak load pricing will cause people who are really at the root of the necessity for capacity expansion to pay the price of that capacity expansion. Why should anybody else pay for it? It's only fair, right?

This is another one of those cases where people worry

about the poor getting screwed. That may or may not be true, but if that's really what you're worried about, why don't you devise a system to help the poor directly? Give them money if you're worried about them being poor, or give them better jobs. This system of pricing will prevent voltage reductions and alternate load sheddings.

Fourth, *make people pay the full social costs of their energy use.* We have had too much pollution in the past, most likely. The reasons are obvious. Air, water, and things like that have been common property. Nobody's cared to take care of them. The result has been that everybody's used them as cesspools. Now the times can change. People are demanding a cleaner environment and are apparently willing to pay for it. This will mean that electric utilities should be charging the full long-run social costs of providing electricity. That might mean a substantial increase in its prices. But why shouldn't the people who use electricity pay for any social damage they cause?* The long-run social costs of providing electricity also would take account of the tremendously increasing costs of capacity expansion, due not only to pollution abatement requirements, but also to general inflationary trends in capital equipment in the rest of the economy. It is socially inefficient to use what are called rolled-in average prices as the mechanism by which one decides what to charge for electricity. The way to social efficiency is to charge people the full cost of what they are using. This way, they take account of the costs they are imposing on society by using the resources. Now, this may mean exorbitant profits for electric utilities. Again, they could be taxed or all excess profits could be put into a trust fund for environmental

---

*The argument is a little more complicated than that, and actually would involve a double system of taxation, both on the pollutor and the pollutee, but those details are not really important here.

control and capacity expansion, or for that matter, to pay off people who suffer from pollution caused by electric utilities. The problem arises here, as always, of the poor getting screwed. The answer is the same. If this is indeed the case, help them out the way they want it most, not by artificially low electricity rates, but by having higher incomes. They obviously can be no worse off, and probably will be better off. Whenever there's a choice to be made about income redistribution, it seems pretty obvious that redistribution in kind could never yield higher utility to the recipients than redistribution by way of universal purchasing power—i.e., money.

Fifth, *recognize the futility of price controls once and for all.* The history of price controls has generally been a history of failure; our last bout with them is no exception. Even those who supported price controls in the beginning started calling for an end to them several years later. No matter what your opinions are on the causes of inflation, the sheer size of the task of controlling prices is enough to ultimately mean their ruin. Nobody can control all the prices in the United States. People have an infinite number of ways of getting around price controls, even oil companies, although they're obviously an easy target for price controllers and that's why we heard so much about them. The product they sell is homogeneous and the companies that produce the product are large and conspicuous. It's not easy to cheat in that situation. However, when gas started getting "short," did you notice something happening? Some of you probably did. You couldn't burn regular gas in your car without the motor knocking. The octane ratings had mysteriously declined during the period of shortages. Did you notice something else? A lot of gas stations didn't give you any service when you filled up, and some of them actually demanded (the nerve!) a 50¢ charge to look under the hood. What were these people doing? Merely responding to an incentive to maximize their own welfare. When the octane rating for gas goes down and the price remains the same, the actual cost per constant quality unit rises. In other words, it's impossible to regulate the real price that people pay for goods and services. You can do it in the short run, and you can cause lots of disruptions in the economy, just as we have seen. In the long run, however, I have faith that human ingenuity will pull us out of any control mechanism. Of course, this expenditure of ingenuity is another major cost of rationing. These efforts could have been directed more usefully in the absence of rationing.

Now don't take this to mean that I'm advocating cheating on price controls. All I'm saying is that people have always cheated, do cheat, and will cheat in the future. And you know what? The more cheating there is, the more efficient the use of resources in this country becomes. Again, however, this is not a plea for disobeying government regulations. It's only a statement about the real world, not the phantasy world imagined by government officials.

Lastly, *divorce foreign policy from economic policy.* Perhaps this is a naive view of what foreign policy is, but it seems to me it all boils down to security, the national kind. Why else do we do all those great magnanimous acts vis à vis other countries? Because we think we're better off, because we think that our national interests are furthered. And when it gets down to the real nitty gritty, our national interests are most importantly involved in national security. The nonsense arguments that were used in the name of national defense to justify the oil import quota system should not have been swallowed by the American public. If we make it very clear what our national defense goals are and the public sees the actual costs of attaining those goals, rational policy decisions can be made. Voters will know the true costs of the military machine. Using various and sundry inefficient, absurd, and sometimes nefarious economic policies in the guise of national defense not only makes national defense more expensive, but it also seems quite demeaning for a great nation; why should the United States involve itself in the petty economic dealings that it has in the past?

Take the example of Mideast oil. If our national defense goals require that we have a certain amount of oil supplies on hand all the time in case of a Middle East blockade, then let's do that, by all means. Pay for that oil storage, above or below the ground. If the Arabs cut us off, we don't have to go whimpering at their feet begging for aid. We don't have to give in to the OPEC cartel in the name of foreign policy. That cartel will break down sooner or later anyway, and if, in fact, we're not relying on the Mideast for "strategic" oil, it would break down even sooner. They wouldn't have the ace up their sleeve that they now think they have.

It is unbelievable the amount of economic policy that is engaged in as part of our foreign policy. Have you ever asked yourself why our government has to be negotiating with other countries in economic dealings? Well, I have, and my only conclusions are the following:

1. Governments can't keep their hands out of anything when they think they can increase their power and prestige.
2. A lot has to do with building economic ties to improve our national defense position—that is to say, to improve our relations with other countries so they will support us during a war.
3. The public believes that only the government can take care of such important matters. It's certainly not obvious that the way they've taken care of these matters

has been in the public's best interest. And, in fact, any model of political bureaucratic action will predict that most, if not all, policy actions will benefit 1) politicians, and 2) special interest groups, but never the general public at large.

The above program really isn't as drastic as it seems. In fact, we're going in that direction already, for example, in the area of natural gas where price has been allowed to rise. By the time you read this, in fact, natural gas may be totally deregulated. We'll eventually get rid of price controls for they certainly haven't been effective at the task they were originally designed to accomplish; prices rose at 8 percent during 1973. Again, by the time you read this, they may be already out.

The important element in this whole discussion is not so much the specific points that have been made. Rather, what is important is your increased awareness of the futility of trying to block natural economic forces in this country or in the world. What governments say they can do and what they say they are doing do not necessarily correspond with what is actually happening. Delve into the issues a little more deeply when a network news commentator or a government official tells you that a crisis is upon the land and the only thing we can do is this, that, or the other thing. Don't automatically agree. If you do, you may be sorry, just as those of us who listened and believed politicians and the media over the past few years are certainly sorry we were so naive.